OF
NAKED LADIES
AND
FORGET-ME-NOTS

Also by Dr. Allan M. Armitage

Dr A has published or edited over 20 books,
here are some of the most popular:

Armitage's Greatest Perennials & Annuals.
An App for smart phones. Updated continuously.

It's Not Just About the Hat

Armitage's Garden Perennials. 2nd ed.

Armitage's Vines and Climbers

The Color Encyclopedia of Garden Plants

Legends in the Garden, Who in the World is Nellie Stevens?
With L.L. Copeland

*Herbaceous Perennial Plants – a treatise on their identification
culture and garden attributes* 3rd ed.

Armitage's Native Plants for American Gardens

Armitage's Garden Annuals. A color encyclopedia

Specialty Cut Flowers, 2nd ed. With J.M. Laushman

Armitage's Manual of Annuals, Biennials and Half-Hardy Perennials

OF
NAKED LADIES
AND
FORGET-ME-NOTS

The stories behind the common names
of some of our favorite plants

Allan M. Armitage

Managing Editor: Katie Elzer-Peters
Content Editor: Polly Brennan
Copy Editor: Billie Brownell
Designer: Nathan Bauer
Proofreader: Shanna Jones

ISBN-13: 978-0-692-85473-0

Printed in the United States of America

Cover Illustration by Linda Fraser, Atlanta, Georgia

Dedication

To my entire family, Susan and I are so blessed.
And a special shout-out to our newest grandchild,
Avery June Armitage. Life is good.

Avery and her best friend Daisy

Acknowledgments

Starting an endeavor like this is easy, but making it come to life requires people who are talented and who believe.

This book would never have seen the light of day without my exceptional editors, Polly Brennan and Katie Elzer-Peters.

And isn't the book cover extraordinary? Thank you, Linda Fraser, for lending us your talent.

I also wish to thank Maria Zampini and Katie Elzer-Peters, every flock needs shepherds, and they shepherded us all through the many steps necessary.

Thank you.

Table of Contents

Some Thoughts of the Author

I have been studying, talking, and teaching about plants for many years. What I've noticed is that what might be the newest, greatest plant today often becomes lost in the shuffle a few years hence. The trendiest gardening fad soon becomes old hat, and the latest volume of *Gardening For Dummies* will appear, letting us all know how complicated gardening has become. I have been involved in this thing we call gardening for over 30 years, and I have always been consistent about one message: gardening should be fun!

I recall speaking at a plant meeting in New York. After the speakers were finished one of the audience members asked, "What do you think of people using common names instead of botanical names?" One of the speakers, a rhododendron guru, stated that he used botanical names exclusively, and the other experts basically said the same. Essentially they stated that common names were confusing and didn't match up in different parts of the country. They felt that as gardeners and landscapers became more competent, using botanical names while speaking or asking for plants wouldn't be a problem.

The audience actually believed this.

As the moderator was about to move on, I couldn't help myself. I said, "Wait a minute, you guys are crazy! Gardeners can't be expected to keep up to date with Latin names! But most importantly, we have to make gardening simpler—and more fun."

I continued to rant. "To think that my daughter Laura is ever going to learn *Chaenomeles* instead of quince, *Baptisia* rather than indigo, and to think she will ever get her tongue around *Calibrachoa* is ludicrous. She hasn't the time or the interest. Of course, we should be using common names. Not as a substitute but as a way of making Laura feel more comfortable."

Suffice it to say, I love common names. And I love telling stories.

"Tell me the facts, I forget. Tell me the story, I remember." I enjoy telling stories and the best are those that people love telling to others. The story of how 'Annabelle' hydrangea came to be, or what a tree had to do with the New York Stock Exchange, or what pinking shears have to do with a plant's name—these stories are all fascinating to me. It turns out they are *also* fascinating to many others.

Some of the most puzzling, yet entertaining, aspects of gardening are the common names of garden plants. So many common names are based in ancient folklore; in fact, very few can be researched in an academic setting because so little information has been published. Some do make sense, particularly those named for similarities to animals (bat face, lion's tail, kangaroo paw), things (bottlebrush, blueberry), or places (Eastern redbud, Canada thistle).

Others, like kiss-me-over-the-garden-gate, love-lies-bleeding, or woundwort, evoke all sorts of quizzical looks. Many common names are based on stories that have survived for years but, without a doubt, successive tellings result in omission, deletion, or addition of a few extra "facts."

So be it. Gardeners can't agree on very much anyway, but the one thing I hope we can all agree on is that this is gardening, not brain surgery or rocket science. So sit back and be amazed, entertained, or astounded while these names come to life.

Disclaimer: I look at this book as I look at history. By its very definition, people whose writings populate history books were often not there at the time. However, based on their research and experience with the subject, their accounts are credible and convincing.

In the case of this book, few references were based on someone being there at the time. Dozens of names may be rooted in an ancient Germanic tongue, found in an Old English dictionary, or buried in an ancient tome on herbology. To be sure, some of the etymology is guesswork, but I have done my best to provide as much credibility as possible to a rather incredible subject.

And oh boy, these common names have been fun to research and even more fun to share. Anyone who takes me to task because some of the information is not academically 100 percent correct should not be reading this book. You do not dream enough.

The first story - Of Naked Ladies and Sleepy Dicks

This was the original title of the book. In fact, when I first told people that I was going to write a book of stories about common names, this was the title I mentioned. It had a certain naughtiness to it, but these were two valid common names of plants we use in our gardens.

However, upon reflection and upon discussion with other smarter people, we decided that it would not make particularly good dinner table discussion. So, we chose the more appropriate title you see on the front cover.

Regardless, the stories of these two plants and many more may be enjoyed within the covers.

Have fun.

A Hydrangea
Named Annabelle

Few plants are known by their cultivar name only. You will find the stories of only three in this book: 'Homestead Purple' verbena, 'Margarita' sweet potato, and here, 'Annabelle' hydrangea.

The story begins in 1910 when sisters Harriet and Amy Kirkpatrick were horseback riding in the countryside near their small town in southern Illinois. They were gardeners, so when they came across a hydrangea unlike any other they had seen, they took a few cuttings. Once they had established them in their own garden, they shared with neighbors. The plants grew and flowered in total anonymity to the rest of the country.

In 1960, fifty years after the sisters' discovery, J.C. McDaniel, a respected woody plant expert from the University of Illinois, happened to travel through the town. He did not recognize the hydrangea that seemed to be growing in every garden there. Fortunately, his curiosity was piqued enough for him to knock on the door of a house whose yard included a couple of these beautiful shrubs. It turned out that he had knocked on the door of Harriet Kirkpatrick's daughter. She had no idea where the hydrangeas came from, just that her mother had found them somewhere.

He asked if he could take some cuttings and three years later, mature plants were ready to be marketed. There was no doubt they would be popular, so a variety name was necessary. It was important that the sisters who found it be honored, and many potential names were bandied about.

The town where the sisters lived was Anna, Illinois, and the name 'Annabelle' honors "The Belles of Anna."

Who would have thought two sisters, a horticulturist, a small town, and a span of over fifty years would result in such an important plant? Although the number of hydrangea cultivars has exploded today, 'Annabelle' is still often listed as one of the top ten shrubs in American horticulture.

'Annabelle' hydrangeas behind daylilies in an Ontario garden

In fact, the mayor of Anna, Illinois, officially designated the second Saturday of June as "Annabelle Day." Pride knows no bounds.

Former Mayor Jim Cross proclaiming Annabelle Day in Anna, Illinois

The Plant

___

Hydrangea arborescens 'Annabelle'   Annabelle hydrangea

'Annabelle' is easy to grow and dependable, performing well from zones 4 to 7. To reduce wilt, plant in a semi-shaded area of the garden and provide abundant water.

To control height and vigor, plants may be cut to the ground during winter. They will still flower the next summer.

References

1. Copeland, Linda L.. and Allan M. Armitage, 2001. _Legends in the Garden – Who in the World is Nellie Stevens?_ Cool Springs Press.

Breathing With The Clouds

I see baby's breath complementing floral designs, tucked into every corsage, and for sale every where cut flowers are sold. Though many modern designers have moved away from baby's breath, it is still sometimes featured in wedding bouquets and congratulatory arrangements for new parents.

The common name seems to have arisen because people who came across plants in the wild described them as "breathing with clouds of tiny white flowers."

In the study of flower meanings, baby's breath is a symbol of everlasting love, pureness, and innocence—all characteristics attributed to babies.

The Plant

Gypsophila paniculata   Baby's breath

While the most popular use for baby's breath is as a cut flower, it is also available as a dwarf edging or ground cover plant in the garden. Smaller cultivars grow only to about a foot but still "breathe" the same white flowers.

Baby's breath requires soils with a basic pH (about 7.0 to 8.0). If you have such soil chemistry, plant away. Otherwise, add some lime to the soil in which plants will be installed. Treat them as annuals or short-lived perennials.

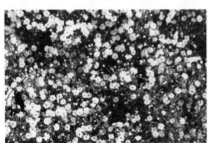

Dwarf baby's breath in a landscape   *Cut baby's breath and roses*

Buttons For Bachelors

Everyone rolls the term "bachelor's buttons" from their tongues when mentioning this plant, so I couldn't help but wonder just who these bachelors were. The more I researched the name, the more confused I became. So, I'll just tell you the story I like best.

The public mores of Victorian England dictated that young men and young women not commingle freely. In fact, even in Colonial America, a chaperone was expected to accompany proper young ladies during evenings out. What was a young man to do?

Bachelor's buttons in a garden with nasturtiums

It turns out that one of the ways a young man could let young ladies know he was "unattached" was to place a certain blue flower discreetly into the buttonhole of his jacket. The flower then became known as bachelor's buttons.

I can't imagine this habit persisted very long; after all, there seems to be a measure of quixotic desperation in the act. Whether this resulted in any amorous encounters is pure conjecture, but it was surely a more refined process than online dating.

Centaurea cyanus   Bachelor's buttons

Native to Europe, plants have escaped to the New World and are common roadside weeds. They may be easily purchased as plants or seeds. They are hardy only to about USDA zone 6, but can reseed almost anywhere. Even in warmer climes, they should be considered a self-sowing annual.

They are excellent for meadow gardens and, as long as other aggressive plants are controlled, they should fill in here and there. In the garden, plant at least three in a group and enjoy their handsome deep blue flowers. They are also excellent as cut flowers to be enjoyed indoors.

Bachelors buttons in a field in Georgia

Stay Away From Baneberry

Many common names evolved from a plant's properties or its parts. The name of this plant is of English provenance. "Bane" indicates that a part of the plant is poisonous, in this case referring to the juice of the berries. Baneberry was first used to describe the European species *Actaea spicata*, which bears black berries.

Baneberry

When the English colonists came to North America and found a similar plant with red berries (*A. rubra*), they simply called it red baneberry.[1] The generally toxic nature of the red baneberry fruit was already well known to Native Americans; they applied the juice to the tips of arrows to impart a secondary and more insidious lethality.[1] Baneberry was also known as red cohosh, from the Algonquin "koshki," meaning rough. The term referred to the gnarled roots of *A. racemosa*, which came to be known as black cohosh. To add to the confusion, the name red cohosh is no longer used for red baneberry.

Our native white-berried plant, *A. pachypoda*, is commonly known as doll's eyes, for obvious reasons.

Red baneberry

The Plant

Actaea   **Baneberry, red baneberry, doll's eyes**

All of the baneberries are
woodland plants, and their
poisonous properties should
eliminate them from use in any
garden setting. You will see them
growing in open woodlands
where the sun penetrates for a
few hours. The white flowers
open in spring, and the fruit
form by summer. Plants are cold
hardy to USDA zone 4.

Doll's eyes

References

1. Hiker's Notebook
http://www.sierrapotomac.org/W_NeedhamBaneberry_100914.htm

Popping Balloons

Balloon flowers have been a mainstay in gardens for years. Not only are they popular for growing, they have long been popular in medicine. Like many other plants, balloon flower was used to ease inflammation, cure infection, and much more. Visiting herbal gardens in places like the Missouri Botanical Garden brings much of the medical history of this plant home.

The common name is one of the more obvious in the plant kingdom. We need only a cursory glance at the expanding flower bud to notice that it puffs up like a balloon before it opens.

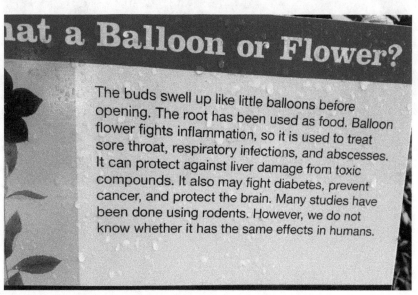

Signage at the Missouri Botanical Garden

If you have a bunch of balloon flowers in the garden and can afford to mess up a few, pick a bulging bud from the plant and squeeze it gently, like you would a tube of toothpaste. The bud will loudly "pop," just like a balloon. The problem is that kids enjoy the popping so much, you may discover that all your buds are deflated because of marauding balloon poppers. Doesn't do much for the garden display.

The Plant

Platycodon grandiflorus   ***Balloon flower***

Plants come in different heights, from nearly 3 feet tall to less than a foot. Check the label before purchasing. The smaller forms are much easier to handle in the garden. Flowers range from the common blue to white and pink. Plant in full sun.

Balloon flower; note the swollen buds among the open flowers

A Balm For Bees

I enjoy growing garden plants that are more than just pretty. The native plant movement and the tremendous interest in pollinators, especially honeybees and butterflies, have encouraged the use of plants that attract them. A plant with the name of bee balm has enjoyed considerable attention from gardeners; after all, who would not want a plant that is a balm for bees?

The problem is, I seldom see bees collecting nectar or happily buzzing around its flowers. And as I look more closely, it is obvious that such an activity would be a virtual impossibility considering the structure of the complex flower.[1]

Scarlet bee balm

However, while plants don't attract bees, the use of a resin derived from the plant may be used for healing and soothing bee stings. The balm, then, is used not for the bees but for humans as a result of encounters with bees.

While the flowers may not attract bees, they certainly seem to be a magnet for hummingbirds.

Monarda species enjoy a number of other common names; the two most familiar are Oswego tea and bergamot. Oswego tea refers to the fact that Native Americans living along the Oswego River watershed made a medicinal brew from the plant.

'Prairie Night' bee balm

Tea from India (one of the British colonies) was a mainstay in Colonial America, and the British started taxing it through acts of Parliament such as the Stamp Act and the Townshend Acts in the late 1760s. People reacted by boycotting British tea, culminating with the infamous Boston Tea Party in 1773. Because of the lack of tea imported from Britain, Oswego tea came into wide use as a substitute.[2]

The name "bergamot" is derived from the fragrance of the leaves, which is similar to bergamot orange (*Citrus bergamia*), the source of bergamot oil. This oil is used to flavor Earl Grey teas, marmalades, and perfumes.

The Plant

Monarda   **Bee balm, Oswego tea, bergamot**

Most of the bee balm sold today is scarlet bee balm, M. *didyma*. A good deal of breeding has resulted in a diversity of flower colors and plant sizes. Plants are handsome and popular, but can become aggressive thugs in the garden. They are also susceptible to powdery mildew; buy resistant varieties. Plant in full sun. They are cold hardy to USDA zone 3.

References

1. Hiker's Notebook
http://www.sierrapotomac.org/W_Needham/BeeBalm_080731.htm
2. USDA Forest Service
http://www.fs.fed.us/wildflowers/plant-of-the-week/monarda_didyma.shtml

Twenty-Four Brokers
And A Buttonwood Tree

I find it most interesting how plants end up in the middle of momentous events, often times in the background, yet integral after the fact. Such an instance became known as the Buttonwood Agreement, resulting in a document with which all students of Economics should be familiar. However I doubt seriously if any of them know what the term "buttonwood" refers to.

Until the late eighteenth century, securities in America were informally brokered in various locations throughout New York City. On May 17, 1792, twenty-four stockbrokers met outside 68 Wall Street hoping to standardize these unregulated transactions.[1] They wished to draft a constitution in which the

Illustration of traders under the buttonwood tree

brokers would agree to deal only with one another, and set a fair and consistent commission in their trades. At that time, a total of five securities were traded in New York City.

Needing a place to gather out of the sun, the signees met under a large buttonwood tree adjacent to that address. Once all had agreed, the document became known as the Buttonwood Agreement. This compact launched the New York Stock

Specimen buttonwood tree

Exchange, today the world's largest with average daily trading of approximately $169 billion in 2013.

The Buttonwood Agreement commemorates the American sycamore (aka buttonwood tree), a plant found from Georgia to Michigan, and west to Missouri. The tree very much lives on in the prestigious magazine *The Economist* (circulation about 1.5 million). One of the columns in each issue is "Buttonwood's notebook" in which financial markets are discussed.

The common name "buttonwood tree" is likely derived from the tree's round fruit, which disperses its seeds in spring, leaving behind only a hard buttonlike core.

There is a mention that sycamore wood was a favorite wood in making buttons at the time1 but I can find no other reference for that.

Bark of a buttonwood tree

The Plant

Platanus occidentalis   Buttonwood tree, American sycamore

This large, North American native tree is easily distinguished by its exfoliating bark, which flakes off in masses, leaving the surface mottled. It can reach 100 feet in height, thus is not a good choice for the suburban garden.

Unfortunately, it is susceptible to anthracnose, rendering it unsightly as a specimen tree. It has been mostly replaced in the landscape by the more resistant London plane tree (*P. x acerifolia*).

References

1. Terrell, Ellen, 2012. History of the New York stock exchange. https://www.loc.gov/rr/business/hottopic/stock_market.html

Who Is That Black-eyed Susan?

I read that the black-eyed Susan is the state flower of Maryland, chosen in part because the colors of the flower matched the colors of the state flag. I admit I was not up on my state flags but when I looked at it, the first colors that assailed me were red and white, hardly the colors of black-eyed Susan. Then I noticed the black and yellow designs in the northwestern and southeastern corners of the flag. It turns out those patterns belonged to George Calvert, the first Lord Baltimore, and reflect his influence founding the colony in 1634.[1]

Maryland state flag

The common name reflects the center of the flower (which is actually more brown than black). However, like so many plants bearing proper names, there is no particular explanation for the name "Susan." Plants are native throughout North America, including in the original 13 colonies. It seems plausible that the original colonists may have named it after someone named Susan.

'Autumn Colors'

Not only is it Maryland's state flower, one of the state's and horseracing's premier events, Baltimore's Preakness Stakes, is called "The Run for the Black-eyed Susans."

'Indian Summer'

The Plant

Rudbeckia hirta   **Black-eyed Susan**

Plants are annuals and widely available at garden centers, or raised from seed. Plant in full sun. They are particularly useful as meadow specimens and associate well with sweet Williams (which see). Dozens of nativars have been bred; many choices await the gardener. Perennial forms, known as yellow coneflowers, are also popular and sometimes known as black-eyed Susans as well.

References

1. Maryland at a glance. Maryland.gov
http://msa.maryland.gov/msa/mdmanual/01glance/html/symbols/flag.html

Bleeding Hearts Everywhere

Every time I see bleeding hearts in someone's garden, they make me want to purchase some for my own (which I do), as well as make me wonder about the common name. "Bleeding hearts" is evocative of several images. Perhaps there is a prince somewhere who fell on his sword or — wait, I digress.

Lady-in-the-bath - do you see her?

One theory suggests that the pink petals represent Cinderella's gown and the white petals are her plain bloomers. Once the white petals are removed, the two parts visible are the glass slippers. The remaining heart breaks into three parts representing the fairy godmother's wand, gold dust, and Cinderella's crown (I cannot make this up!). While this may be an interesting story, it does not explain where the name came from.

Actually, this is a simple one. Look at the flowers hanging down like clothes on a clothesline. Each flower is in the shape of a heart, and the pistil looks like it is bleeding, albeit white blood, but bleeding nevertheless.

Bleeding heart

Another common name is lady-in-the-bath, apparently referring to the "lady" represented by the inner petals and pistil when the flower is flipped upside down. The outer pink petals are the bath. I never made the connection, but it seems that others have. It is kind of cool, but way too much work to show it off.

'Gold Heart'

Lamprocapnos spectabilis   **Bleeding heart**

We all originally learned the plant as *Dicentra spectabilis* but the name has recently been changed. This plant is a wonderful shade tolerant addition to the garden. Flowers appear in spring and a number of fine choices are available. My favorite by far is 'Gold Heart'. It has chartreuse foliage that contrasts well with the pink flowers. Plants are hardy to USDA zone 4. Plants will likely go dormant during summer but emerge fresh the next year.

The Bloody Bloodroot

I have always been enamored with bloodroot. Not only is it a handsome native plant, beautiful in the wild or in my garden, but it is a plant I always show people in my "walkabouts." Kids, adults, and 80-year-old grandmas get on their knees while I dig and snap the root of the plant. The bloody sap soon tells the story behind its common name. All are excited to see it but before I can move on to the next plant, I must rescue the grandmas still trying to get up.

The cut root of bloodroot

The name obviously comes from the blood-red sap, used by Native American tribes for dyeing clothing, baskets, or occasionally as skin paint. However, stories of widespread use of bloodroot for painting skin are dubious as many people are quite allergic to the sap, which can cause blisters and dermatitis.

Extracts obtained from bloodroot contain sanguinarine, used in dental hygiene products. The United States FDA has approved the inclusion of sanguinarine in toothpastes as an antibacterial or anti-plaque agent.

Another common name for the plant is puccoon, although that name is not so common anymore. Puccoon likely comes from the seventeenth century Virginia Algonquian word "poughkone," and was recorded by early Virginia settlers to mean red dye or red paint.[1] Interestingly, puccoon was used for other plants that yielded red color, such as pokeweed (which see).

The Plant

Sanguinaria canadensis   *Bloodroot, puccoon*

This is one of the easiest wildflowers to grow, at least in Canada and the Northeast, Midwest, and Southeast in the United States. The hardest part is getting started as they are relatively expensive to buy. The best way is to ask your garden friends if you could liberate a few plants from their garden. Plants are cold hardy to USDA zone 3.

Flowers of bloodroot in the spring

Place in well-drained soils in a location with afternoon shade. Plants will spread in a few years. Once they are established in the garden, feel free to occasionally dig out a root and then break it to show others a little bit of American history.

References

1. Merriam Webster Dictionary. Puccoon
http://www.merriam-webster.com/dictionary/puccoon

Does Boneset Really Set Bones?

Boneset is native to much of eastern North America, including western Massachusetts, the home of Joe Pye weed (which see). Plants were used by Native Americans to induce copious sweating to help break fevers. The name was likely derived from the plant's ability to treat breakbone fever (dengue fever), a condition that causes debilitating pain in the bones. The treatment calmed the screaming limbs, and so the plant name became known as boneset.

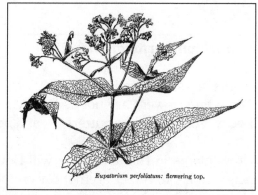

Eupatorium perfoliatum: flowering top.

Boneset drawing showing perfoliated leaves

A poultice made of the plant was used as a wrap around broken appendages in the belief it could help set the bone. There was no proof of its efficacy, but the plant may have obtained its common name this way.

Boneset in a meadow

Another story suggests that the name arose from the belief that the plant was useful as a treatment for pertussis (whooping cough) and relieved the jarring cough that "would make the bones ache." As above, there is little evidence to support the efficacy of this plant as a cough suppressant, but oftentimes efficacy is not a prerequisite for belief.

The Plant

Eutrochium perfoliatum   **Boneset**

Plants are seen mostly in native plantings or meadow gardens. The white flowers are not as showy as those of its cousin, Joe Pye weed, but attract butterflies and bees *en masse.*

Grow plants in full sun. They will flower in late summer and heights of 4 to 5 feet are not uncommon. The genus has been changed from *Eupatorium*, which we all knew and loved, to *Eutrochium.*

Cleaning The Ale Glasses
With Bouncing Bet

This popular perennial is also known as soapwort as it was one of the first plants used as soap as far back as medieval times. It became popular as a cleaning agent in inns, pubs, and anywhere eating and drinking dishes required washing.

Bouncing Bet

Apparently, barmaids in England were at one time referred to as "Bets." They cleaned bottles by adding a sprig or two of the plant to some water already in the bottle and shaking vigorously. Perhaps, after a few too many drinks, the boys in the bar came to know the women as "bouncing Bets." The name of the plant became synonymous with its use. That may seem like quite a fable but most stories I find are based on the same pub tales.

Not to give barmaids all the credit, others speculate that the shape and structure of the flower parts suggest the juggling rump of a laundress. I have tried to make the connection, but I don't buy it. Then again, I don't know any laundresses.

The Plant

Saponaria   Bouncing Bet

Both *S. officinalis* and the shorter *S. ocymoides* have been useful in making soap and both are known as soapwort. The former can get quite weedy and aggressive and may reach 8 to 12 inches in height. The latter, rock soapwort or bouncing bet, is low growing (less than a foot tall) and is excellent for sunny rock gardens. Rock soapwort is useful as a groundcover, and quite wonderful when allowed to flow down the sides of mixed containers.

They are cold hardy to about USDA zone 3, but do poorly in warm climates warmer than zone 7.

The Eye-Catching Myth
Of The Carrot

Ever since I gave up bread and muffins as evening snacks, I have been munching on mini carrots and ranch dressing. I know carbohydrate consumption causes weight gain, so the low carbs of the lowly carrot made sense. Of course, the real problem is that I simply can't watch television without munching on something. Pathetic, I know.

I also accepted this carrot fate because, as everyone knows, the high vitamin A content in carrots improves your vision, especially night vision. So while my taste buds and stomach might suffer, I figure my vision would surely improve. Turns out that is not so.

While vitamin A is generally beneficial for eye health, carrots do nothing to improve vision. It turns out this faulty theory about carrots was actually popularized by the British Ministry of Information in World War II. The myth was creative subterfuge to mislead German aircraft preparing to bomb in World War II.

CARROTS
keep you healthy and help you
to see in the blackout

The Germans were intent on releasing bombs on English cities and did so most often at night. However, in 1940, the English started using new radar technology that allowed Allied planes to intercept German aircraft over the English Channel, even at night. According to The Imperial War Museum and the UK National Archives, the new technology was to be kept under tight wraps. The Ministry told the daily newspapers that their pilots had superior night vision—the result of eating carrots.[1]

No one really knows if the Germans were fooled, but many British citizens definitely were, and the myth was celebrated. Because of constant blackouts, people were encouraged by the government to eat carrots to improve vision.

The British government even embarked on a "Doctor Carrot" campaign to boost consumption, and left carrots untouched by wartime food rations, giving further credibility to the deception. During

my research, I discovered the existence of the World Carrot Museum online.[2] Really neat!

Carrots may be nutritious, but they really won't help you pass your vision test or find your glasses in the dark. They sure mess up my diet, though.

Ready to harvest!

Carrots for sale at a farmers' market

The Plant

Daucus carota   *Carrot*

Unless your soil is sandy loam, raised beds are best for growing carrots. The more clay in your soil, the greater the need for raised beds. Use transplants if available to reduce the problems of seed propagation. If sowing seed, direct sow 3 to 5 weeks before your area's first frost date. Plant in full sun and fertilize 5 to 6 weeks after sowing. Carrots reach maturity 2 to 3 months after they emerge.

There are many fine cultivars; my favorites are 'Inverness' and 'Danvers Half Long'. If you want some fun, try the colored forms like 'Purple Dragon' or the rounder roots of 'Parmex Baby Ball'.

References

1. Smith, A.K., 2013. *A WWII propaganda campaign popularized the myth that carrots help you see in the dark.* Smithsonian.com
http://www.smithsonianmag.com/arts-culture/a-wwii-propaganda-campaign-popularized-the-myth-that-carrots-help-you-see-in-the-dark-28812484/?no-ist
2. The World Carrot Museum. www.worldcarrotmuseum.com

Waiting An Entire Century For Flowers

Every year, and almost monthly in the summer, headlines in local papers trumpet that Miss Winbus's or Dr. Bruganti's or Mr. Smith's century plant is about ready to bloom. It is heralded as a once-in-a-lifetime event, worthy of television reporters, festivals, and parades. When I Googled "century plant stories" I was assailed by a dozen breathless features from Arizona, Texas, Florida, California, and Kentucky. The reality is not quite so amazing.

Century plant almost in flower, El Charco del Ingenio Botanical Garden, San Miguel de Allende, Mexico

Plants are slow to grow, slow to mature, and therefore slow to bloom. The common name refers to the long time they take to flower. Actually, they require anywhere between 5 to 15 years to send up their huge flowering stems, depending on the environment and the vigor of the individual plant. That is certainly slow, but they are not literally century plants. And then, after all that, the mother plant dies. But offsets remain.

The Plant

Agave americana   **Century plant**

This is a fun plant to try growing, and is excellent for hot, dry areas. Remember that once it starts flowering, the flower stalk can grow to well over 20 feet in height. All of the nutrients for flowering have been stored over the many years the plant remained vegetative, and once on its way, the flowering stem can grow a foot a day. In fact, greenhouse and conservatory operators sometime have to remove parts of a roof so the flower stem achieves its complete length.

Leaves are sharp and vicious, not at all child or eyeball friendly. Plants are cold hardy to about USDA zone 8; other species of agave are significantly hardier.

Flowering stems of century plants, Canary Islands

Who Knew Chastity Grew On Trees?

As you might guess, many interesting stories are associated with this name. As far back as the second century, Roman writers such as Pliny the Elder and Dioscorides suggested that *Vitex* could be used to curb sexual desire. Pliny reported the use of stems and leaves of this plant as bedding for women "to cool the heat of lust." As such, chaste tree is known as an anaphrodisiac.

Another common name is monk's pepper, which arose in medieval times when the peppercorn-like fruit of the tree was recommended to monks to blunt their libido, thus helping them maintain their vows of chastity.

The "chaste-enhancing" properties of *Vitex* have essentially been debunked but extracts are available over the counter, usually under the name chaste tree berry, to ease symptoms of premenstrual syndrome.

The Plant

Vitex agnus-castus   *Chaste tree*

Vitex is a small tree, often used as an ornamental flowering street specimen, growing 10 to 15 feet tall. The lilac-purple flowers open in late spring to early summer. Plants are excellent for hot climates and are commonly seen in the Southeast and Southwest but seldom in the North. It's hardy to USDA zone 6, although in zone 5 plants may survive but suffer significant dieback.

After flowering, small black small black berries appear, and trees also became known as chasteberry trees.

A handsome chaste tree in flower

Did The Confederacy Really Have A Rose?

I saw a Confederate rose for the first time on a late October day in Athens, Georgia. It was well over 7 feet tall and bore immense, double pink flowers. It looked a bit like a hibiscus and when I asked my southern friend what it was, he looked at me pitifully and said, "Don't you know that's a Confederate rose?" I had so much to learn.

Common double flowers of Confederate rose

I suppose at first glance the flower does look a little like a rose, especially the common double forms, but the closer you get, the less rosy it appears. The name probably resulted from the fact that plants were so common in the Confederate States of America during the nineteenth century that it was adopted as their "rose."

From 1861–1865, the breakaway region known as the Confederate States consisted of South Carolina, Mississippi, Florida, Alabama, Georgia, Louisiana, and Texas. These plants are still prevalent and popular in those states.

The Plant

Hibiscus mutabilis   **Confederate rose**

Plants are cold hardy only to USDA zones 7 or 8. If perennial, they break through the soil later in spring than most perennials (like all hibiscus), and then grow rapidly. They make poor annuals in the North because they are so late to bloom that hard frosts usually kill them before buds can open.

However, they are quite handsome in flower, and selection has provided gardeners with single- and double-flowered forms. Flowers often change color as they mature (the species name of *mutabilis* means to mutate).

Take My Breath Away

Pleurisy is a condition in which the lining of the lungs (pleura) and the chest wall become inflamed. It is often associated with fluid accumulation between the lung linings. Some of the symptoms include chest pain during inhalation, tenderness in the chest, and particularly shortness of breath.

Pleurisy was far more common in the days before antibiotics. Today, it is not uncommon, but most cases are the result of viral infections, and deaths are rare. This was not always the case. Notable pleurisy sufferers included Charlemagne (the father of Europe), Catherine de Medici, Benjamin Franklin, William Wordsworth, Tad Lincoln (the youngest son of Abraham Lincoln), Mahatma Gandhi, and Rudolf Valentino. It is no wonder that physicians scoured the plant world to find a treatment.

Pleurisy root, butterfly weed in Burlington, Ontario

In the New World, a species of milkweed (*Asclepias*) was found to be effective in treating pleurisy. The dried roots were used by Native Americans as a remedy for pulmonary infections;[1] modern physicians seized upon the plant and used it to treat many lung issues, including pleurisy and pneumonia. And so it became known as pleurisy weed or pleurisy root. Pleurisy root was an official medicine in the United States Pharmacopoeia from 1820 to 1905.[1]

Butterfly weed is a far more common name, referring to the fact that the flowers are a primary source of food for many butterflies, most notably the monarch.

The Plant

Asclepias tuberosa   *Pleurisy root, butterfly weed*

As much as I love seeing butterflies float over these flowers in my garden, it is not an easy plant to establish in many settings. They're far more successful when left alone along roadsides or in sunny meadows. They transplant poorly and many plants are lost in gardens due to too much love and care. They are also late to emerge, and can fall victim to overly exuberant weeding.

Pleurisy root is not nearly as common in nature as it was decades ago, and this fact, among others, has resulted in a decline of monarch butterflies. That is an excellent reason for gardeners to establish plants in urban and suburban gardens. If you do so, buy established plants; do not dig them from the wild! Then place them in an open sunny area with excellent drainage—they abhor "wet feet." Once established, they provide eye-popping color for you, and a source of food for butterflies.

References

1. Vogel VJ. *American Indian Medicine*. Norman: University of Oklahoma Press, 1970:287-8

Little Lambs Eat Ivy

When one is looking for a silver accent in a garden, the first plant they'll see mentioned in every design book and perennial catalog is lamb's ears. We all know it and we all grow it. The common name is pretty straightforward. The soft cuddly leaves reminded early herbalists of the ear of a lamb. It was also known as rabbit's ears and donkey's ears.

The genus *Stachys* is known as betony, from the Celtic words "bew" (a head) and "ton" (good), "it being healing for complaints of the head."[1] The other popular common name for lamb's ears is woolly betony.

Lamb's ears at the front of a garden

Stachys byzantina   *Lamb's ears*

Plants may be placed in full sun in the North, but in the South, a little afternoon shade allows for better performance. They do best in dry climates; too much rain and humidity usually result in poor-looking plants by midsummer. Cultivars such as 'Helene von Stein' are more adaptable to inclement conditions.

References

1. Grieve, M. 1931. *A Modern Herbal*, Harcourt, Brace & Co

'Helene von Stein' lamb's ears

How a Voodoo Lily
Almost Canceled A Marriage

Does anyone have a Heather in your life? Our middle child, Heather, was born irascible, and as she grew it seemed that she was the only one in control of anything. If you wanted to know the weather, Heather could tell you. If you wanted something done, give it to Heather. For Heather, it was always her way or no way.

Don't get me wrong; she was a wonderful daughter—no serious trouble at school or with her friends, her grades were fine, and she was kind to others. We loved her dearly, but oh my, she was simply "Heather" at every turn, a drama queen at every opportunity. We divorced at least 4 times, but we all survived—barely.

Does Heather remind you of anyone in your family?

Then, one day, after finishing her degree in nursing, Heather came home and announced, "Somebody wants to marry me!"

The notorious "almost engagement breaking" voodoo lily in the Armitage garden

Yes!!!

Susan and I readied the house and garden for a visit from the future in-laws. Heather filled us in; they were good Southern Baptists, really nice people. That was not much to go on, but Susan polished and scrubbed and I weeded and edged. We hid the beer and liquor, and we even straightened the pictures—we were not going to mess this up.

The morning prior to the visit was relatively calm, until I heard Heather call me frantically from the back deck. "Dad, Dad! Something stinks out here. I think something died!" Sure enough, a grim odor permeated the air. And that is when I realized it— my voodoo lily had opened that morning.

I am the first to admit that this is a rather bawdy-looking to downright ugly plant. However, every beetle and bug, every fly and gnat in the entire county was loving this flower, and having their convention right before us. Its other common name, carrion lily, seemed apropos at that moment. Personally, I thought it was pretty cool but Heather was beside herself. We passed each other in the kitchen, me going for my camera, Heather going for the scissors.

I tried to mollify her with my horticulture doublespeak about pollinators and ecosystems, but she was having none of it. However I calmed her down by suggesting that this unique plant may be interesting to our guests, and quietly prayed that the wind would be blowing away from us. I did not feel that the voodoo lily would be grounds for breaking an engagement; Heather was not so sure.

The company arrived; we drank our tea, ate our cookies, and wandered around the house and garden. Heather kept trying to steer them away from the back deck, but once there, they were as fascinated with the voodoo lily as I was. All went quite splendidly, but not without drama. To this day, when I see a voodoo lily, I think of that time, and smile.

A brief epilogue: Heather and David have been married for 12 years and are doing very well. Their first son arrived about 2 years after they were married, and somehow, three more children (twin boys and a daughter) arrived soon thereafter. So soon, in fact, that Heather was scrambling to care for four children under the age of 5. Yes, there is a God!

 The Plant

Dracunculus vulgaris   ***Voodoo lily***

Bulbs can be planted in a shady location and, if sufficiently large, will flower the first year. They are in the Jack-in-the-pulpit family and when the flowers emerge, will consist of a shiny purple spathe and spadix (see Preaching with Jack).

The name voodoo lily is appropriate for this somewhat shadowy flower. They are cold hardy to about USDA zone 7, though a dear friend successfully overwintered one for several years in zone 5. Plants generally grow 3 feet tall and emit the odor of dead meat, thus are also known as carrion lily. All I can say if you choose to grow this is, "Have fun."

The Peeling Crape Myrtle

Every now and then I wonder what in the world I did uprooting my family from Montreal and ending up in the South, the land of kudzu, pokeweed, and boiled peanuts. While I have yet to emphatically embrace any of these uniquely Southern charms, I have come to love the crape myrtle. From June to August, the land is alive with the blossoms of this extraordinary Chinese expatriate. The common name causes a bit of head scratching though. The leaves may be mistaken for those of myrtle but the "crape" part is a little puzzling.

This plant was introduced to England from China in 1759, but it did not impress many people there. The problem was that few regions in England were warm enough to support the vigorous growth for which crape myrtle is now known.

However, around 1786, the French botanist, Andre Michaux (1746-1802) brought plants to Charleston, SC. They flourished. They have become the summer-flowering tree of the South, and extend well up into the Mid-Atlantic states.

The common name probably arose not for the constitution of the flowers but for the bark, which peels off in thin sheets over the season, and was often compared to crepe paper. In fact, the bark is probably the most ornamental part of the tree because it is as handsome in winter as it is in summer.

A continuing argument concerns the spelling of "crape." After all, the term comes from the Old French

Peeling bark of crape myrtle

word *crespe*, changed to "crêpe" in the eighteenth century. So why is the name not spelled crepe myrtle? Dozens of names have been translated to other languages, resulting in slightly different spellings, so this would not be puzzling. However, there was no love lost between the English and French in those times, and it was just as likely that the English wouldn't accept "crêpe" simply because it was French.

Crape myrtles, Athens, Georgia

Lagerstroemia indica   **Crape myrtle**

Today, one can find plants in a wide spectrum of heights, ranging from 3-foot shrubs to 25-foot trees. Flower colors are available in almost any hue.

Place plants in full sun and water in well. If growing as a tree, remove bottom branches as the plant matures. This will make the handsome peeling bark more obvious.

What Does Dame's Rocket Have To Do With Vegetables?

Dame's rocket is loved and reviled with equal intensity. Those who love it comment on its evening fragrance, its handsome flower color, and the ease of growing. The other camp describe the invasiveness of the plant and do all in their power to remove it.

The botanical name, *Hesperis matronalis*, provides a hint to the common name. *Hesperis* means "of the evening," perhaps named because of the evening fragrance of the flowers. *Matronalis*, "of matrons," likely again refers to a lady's use of perfumes.

Dame's violet and mother-of-the-evening are other common names referring to women, but why a rocket? Rockets, as we know them today, certainly did not exist when the plants were first named. It turns out that the name might have come from a vegetable.

Dame's rocket

The genus *Hesperis* is in the mustard family; the young leaves are rich in vitamin C and can be eaten raw as a cress substitute in salads. One of the prominent members of the family is arugula, a plant quite similar in leaf to *Hesperis*. The old French name for arugula, still used in many seed catalogs today, is "roquette." It is likely the English simply took liberties with the French name and "dame's rocket" was coined.

The Plant

Hesperis matronalis   **Dame's rocket**

Dame's rocket is abundant in the Midwest, Northeast, and in southeast Canada. It is a handsome meadow plant or a pernicious roadside weed, depending on your point of view. There is no doubt about its invasive qualities—seeds are abundantly produced and dispersed. In fact, one reason it is so plentiful is that many "wildflower mix" seed packets include dame's rocket.

To be sure, I would not recommend planting it in the garden unless vigilance is your middle name. Plants are cold hardy to USDA zone 3; they do poorly in the South.

The Dusty Miller

If there is another plant name as confusing as dusty miller, I would like to know. At least four genera have members commonly sold as dusty miller, including *Senecio, Cineraria, Artemisia,* and *Jacobaea.* The only things these dusty millers have in common are the gray color and hairy texture of their somewhat dusty-looking leaves.

The common name arose in the early nineteenth century and refers to the fine powder on the leaves, perhaps an allusion to a miller, who, by definition, is always dusty.

The common bedding plant referred to as dusty miller received a name change from *Senecio cineraria* to *Jacobaea maritima.* The genus *Jacobaea* is chock-full of plants with interesting common names such as stinking willie/nanny/ninny, staggerwort, cankerwort, stammerwort, mare's fart, and cushag. As I read these names again, I once again understand that discretion is the better part of valor. I won't go there.

Dusty miller with 'Winter Red' holly

The Plant

Jacobaea maritima   *Dusty miller*

The woolly leaves provide excellent contrast to other plants in garden beds and mixed containers. In most of the country, plants should be used as annuals; in frost-free areas, they may become woody and shrublike.

Plant in full sun.

Making The Pig Squeal

I have been talking about plants to different audiences for many years. I speak about new plants, flowering plants, foliage plants, perennials, annuals, and on and on. During one of my first forays into storytelling, I decided to talk about *Bergenia*, a vigorous leather-leaved perennial plant with handsome pink flowers. After showing a slide or two on the screen, I went on to suggest that the common name, pigsqueak, was more user-friendly than bergenia or its other common name, elephant ears.

I softened up the audience by telling them how anyone will forever remember the plant with just a simple story. I arranged the microphone and proceeded to explain that if you rub the leaf between your thumb and forefinger just right, you can hear a pig squeal.

Pigsqueak plants

I began my demonstration. I reached into my back pocket and whipped out the bergenia leaf I had liberated from a plant forty five minutes previously.

Up-close pigsqueak flowers

The room was hushed as I whispered, "Just like this," and rubbed the leaf. . . and. . . nothing happened. I tried again. "Just like this." Silence—except for chuckles from the audience. I glanced down and quickly realized I had cut it too early before my talk. A limp leaf tells no tales; its squealing days were done.

This was not one of my more credible moments. However, I went to the garden later with a group of believers, and, on my knees, I rubbed a turgid leaf and made the pig squeal. People were delighted, I was relieved, and pigs have been squealing all over the country ever since.

By the way, I think the common name pigsqueak should be changed to pigsqueal. Once you do this with a few bergenia leaves, you will probably agree.

The Plant

Bergenia spp.   *Pigsqueak*

Piqsqueak is a common plant in the northern states and southern Canada, but not so much in the southern half of the country. Best known for their leathery dark leaves, plants are often used as edging plants around garden beds. Protect from afternoon sun and provide water as needed. In spring, handsome pink flowers emerge. Useful in USDA zones 4 to 7.

The Old Man And His Beard

Many names are given to various species of clematis and nearly all are impossible to trace to their origins. Some of the better-known include traveler's joy, virgin's bower, and even orange peel plant. Fortunately, most gardening people simply call them clematis, which comes from Greek, meaning "a climbing plant." Were all names that easy!

Many clematis produce beautiful fluffy seed heads, a feature often overshadowed by the hundreds of glossy photos of bigger and bigger flowers in today's catalogs. The fuzzy congestion of the seeds resulted in the common name of old man's beard. I think it is quite apropos, don't you?

Fruit of many clematis actually do resemble an old man's beard

Another well-known name for clematis is virgin's bower. This was originally given to *C. viticella*, a species native to the Mediterranean region. Plants were brought into common cultivation in England during the reign of Queen Elizabeth I, "the virgin queen," and the common name likely pays homage to her. Much later, the same name was given to the American native

C. virginiana. This looks nothing like the true virgin's bower and actually may refer to the state of Virginia, where it is native.

Traveler's joy refers to the British native *C. vitalba*, for growing alongside many well-traveled paths.

The Plant

Clematis   *Old man's beard, virgin's bower*

In nearly all cases, clematis are climbers or at least ramblers. They may be grown on trellises (bowers) or through shrubs and trees. Flowers ranging from 1 to 6 inches wide are available and colors cover almost every hue of the rainbow. Species may be native to Asia, Europe, or North America.

Most clematis tolerate full sun; they simply need to be well watered the first year to establish. Many species are cold hardy to USDA zone 3, others only to zones 7 or 8.

Diversity of clematis, 'Rooguchi' and 'Huldine'

The Doctrine
Of Signatures

The common names of plants often seem to have no rhyme or reason. While some arise from folklore, often with little basis in today's reality, others are the result of theological and herbal studies. One of the more intriguing theories about plants resulted from a respected herbalist who believed that plants looked somewhat human.

The Greek botanist Pedanius Dioscorides (40-90 AD) served as a medic in the Roman army, and penned the five-volume herbal encyclopedia *De Materia Medica* around 60 AD. In it, he suggested that herbs that resemble parts of the body might be used in treating that body part.[1]

Paracelsus *by Quentin Matsys*   *Pedanius Dioscorides*

Dioscorides's concepts appeared occasionally in writing but it wasn't until the 16th century that his ideas were given credence. Philippus Aureolus Bombastus von Hohenheim, otherwise known as Paracelsus (1493–1541) was a brilliant physician and astrologer. He is credited as the founder of toxicology. He utilized observations from nature, not from just ancient texts, a radical departure of the time. He wrote and lectured about herbal uses of plants and trumpeted his belief in what became known as The Doctrine of Signatures. The names of many of the plants we grow today resulted from his writings.[2]

The theologian William Coles (1626–1662) later justified Pacacelsus's ideas by saying that God wanted to show man what plants would be useful for healing. Others followed Paracelsus and the doctrine was accepted well into the seventeenth century.

What In The World Is A Wort?

Many plants seem to carry this designation, and one can quite fairly wonder, "What is a wort?" Several plants bearing this term have something to do with parts or ailments of the body. The term "wort," although meaning only an herb or plant, has come to designate a plant that is "useful for" or "aids in."

Based on on Peracelsus's doctrine, a number of plants were named based on body parts. Here are some examples.

Lungwort: *Pulmonaria*
The spots on the leaves of *Pulmonaria* seemed to look like the alveoli of the lungs. Thus it was used to treat the respiratory problems and became known as lungwort.

The spots on the leaves on Pulmonaria resulted in the common name lungwort

OF NAKED LADIES AND FORGET-ME-NOTS

Liverwort: *Hepatica*

Because *Hepatica* has three lobes on the leaves, it is thought to resemble the lobes of the liver. Plants were used to treat ailments of that organ and became known as liverwort.

The three leaf lobes of hepatica resulted in the common name liverwort

Spleenwort: *Asplenium*

These ferns have spleen-shaped spore cases on the back of the fronds, and plants were recommended for ailments of the spleen.

Beneath the fronds are the spleen-like spore cases

<u>Toothwort:</u> *Cardamine*
Early botanists described the plant's rhizomes as resembling teeth, and plants were prescribed to treat toothaches.

None of these so called "wort" plants had any efficacy on the parts of the body they were supposed to heal, but The Doctrine of Signatures and the common names that resulted are a part of our gardening history.

Toothwort, an American native plant

By the way, what plant or plant part do you think was thought to heal "aches of the brain?" The walnut, of course.

Other "worts" not associated with The Doctrine of Signatures include:

Spiderwort: *Tradescantia*
Spiderwort was not used to treat spider bites as the name would imply but was thought to refer to the fact that the thin stamens of the flower resemble spider legs.

'Sylvanna' spiderwort

Soapwort: *Saponaria officinalis*
This was one of the first plants to be used as soap. It turns out that the leaves and roots abound in saponin and produce froth when rubbed in water. Also see bouncing Bet.

Soapwort growing in a Quebec herb garden

St. John's Wort: *Hypericum*

This is probably the most famous "wort" of all. Legend tells us that in the first century, early Christians were credited for naming St. John's wort after their beloved John the Baptist. The brightly colored flowers open around June 24, which is celebrated as his birthday (see more under St. John's wort).

The most famous "wort" of all is St John's wort

References

1. Dioscorides, P. AD 50-70. De Materia Medica. Translated to English, 1655.
2. Doctrine of signatures. http://www.sciencemuseum.org.uk/broughttolife/techniques/doctrine

What Do Dogwoods Have To Do With dogs?

I can't imagine anyone who has ever seen a dogwood in all its glory doesn't wonder, just a little bit, what in the world this tree has to do with dogs. I suppose it is not something anyone dwells on—but dogs?

A possible explanation for the "dog" name is that the bark of a dogwood was boiled to create a resulting liquid used to treat mange on dogs. However, I believe this is an example of a story based on the name rather than an explanation of the name. There is no active medicinal ingredient in dogwood bark. It is likely that the dogwood name suggested it must be good for dogs, so dogs were bathed in the liquid.

Kousa dogwood in Champaign, Illinois

The most sensible interpretation has to do with the hardness of the wood. The common name likely evolved over time from the Old English word "dagwood." The slender stems of its very hard wood were used for "dags" (daggers, skewers, and arrows). Apparently, sometime in the early 1600s, dagwood was changed to dogwood.

The Plant

Cornus spp.   *Dogwood*

There are well over forty species of dogwoods, most grown for their handsome bracts, others for their winter bark. The most common in this country are our native flowering dogwood, *C. florida*, and the Asian species, *C. kousa*.

The Asian dogwood is more cold hardy but less heat tolerant than the native dogwood, and flowers 2 to 4 weeks later. In the North, plant in full sun; in the South, some afternoon shade results in better longevity. Dogwoods are cold hardy to about USDA zone 5.

Flowering dogwood in Athens, Georgia

Do Only Dutchmen Wear Breeches?

This wonderful native ephemeral has many names. Some include stagger weed (due to a narcotic in the foliage), bleeding heart, eardrops, fairy candles, and little boys' breeches. The small white flowers are easily recognized but they persist only about 10 days. They are best seen while enjoying a spring walk in the woods.

Breeches are simply short pants generally tighten just below the knee. They were popular attire until the early 1900s in western Europe, particularly in Holland. They have long gone out of favor as everyday wear but are still popular today for equestrian sports.

The blooms hang from the pink flower stem like breeches on a clothesline, thus the common name. The flowers are a composite of four petals: two folding upward to form the "legs," the other two tucked inside.

Dutchman's breeches in a woodland garden

The Plant

Dicentra cucullaria   **Dutchman's breeches**

Plants may be purchased from native plant nurseries and bulb specialists, often as dormant tubers. They are difficult to grow from seed, although they will sometimes reseed in the garden if you're very lucky.

Place in an area with dappled sunshine, perhaps under a canopy of deciduous trees. In early spring they produce exquisite fernlike foliage, with the "breeches" appearing soon after. Plants go dormant by late spring.

How Did A Vegetable Become An Egg?

I admit to food illiteracy. I am one of those who eats to live, not the other way around. So while I enjoy a fine gourmet meal, I am quite content to eat a homemade chef salad while watching *60 Minutes*. I am sure there are psychologists who study why some foods are more appealing than others, but the name of the food is probably involved somewhere. I suppose "bubble and squeak," "head cheese," or "toad in a hole" are lovable terms to foodies but for the "eat to live" people, not so much.

White eggplant with flower

It is that way with eggplant. How did this elongated purple member of the tomato family become associated with an egg? It turns out every foodie knows that purple eggplants are historically rather new; in fact, eggplants were usually white— and round—like an egg! The term "eggplant" was first recorded in 1767 for cultivars that were small, round, and yellow or white. It appears the first recorded purple eggplant fruit did not appear until the early 1900s.[1] Now that I am no longer illiterate, bring on the eggplant Parmesan.

Eggplants are also referred to as aubergines, particularly in the United Kingdom. The name was borrowed from the French word *aubergine* or the Catalan *alberginia*, essentially translating to fruit of the eggplant. The term "aubergine" has now come to mean "a particular dark purple color" as well.

Eggplant on the deck

The Plant

Solanum melongena   ***Eggplant***

Eggplants are among the most attractive vegetables for the container on the deck or in the garden. The striking flowers are lilac blue or white and, even if they do not produce fruit, plants are sufficiently handsome to stand on their own.

Fruit can be purple, striped, and of course white, and round or elongated. Plant in full sun, water well, and enjoy your eggplant soufflé.

References

1. Maerz, A. and M.R. Paul. 1930. A dictionary of color. McGraw Hill, New York

An Eye For An Eye, A Tooth For A Tooth

Certain plants simply light up peoples' faces—they may be fun to look at, fun to show to others, and are sometimes even fun to taste. Eyeball plant has it all.

Two common names are often used for this one; the first is eyeball plant. There are no magic potions, wood nymphs, or stories steeped in legend to explain the common name—the flowers simply stare back at you.

Eyeballs staring back

Toothache plant is the other common name, based on the fact that the leaves and flowers cause significant salivation when chewed. Dental professionals often mention salivation as important for tooth health. The chemical spilanthol has been isolated from these plants. Some people swear by a daily mouth rinse of an extract from eyeball plant to promote gum health. They claim chewing as little as a single bud of the plant can numb the mouth and reduce the pain of toothache for up to 20 minutes depending on the sensitivity of the pain.[1]

Research has resulted in the production and marketing of an increasing number of personal and health care products using this plant, as well as items for culinary use. Various plants in the genus are used for their anti-inflammatory, hepatoprotective, and diuretic properties, and to treat a wide range of disorders like toothache, gastritis, gastric ulcers, mucous membrane inflammation, burns, and wounds.[2] And you thought this was just a simple garden plant.

Eyeball plants in full flower

I always take my students and other unwary folks to the patch of eyeball plant in the garden. After the oohing and aahing about the eyeballs, I invite a few of the more hardy souls to taste a small bit of a leaf. Soon they comment on the numbness and the copious saliva that begins flowing. Great spitting, great fun.

The Plant

Spilanthes acmella   **Eyeball plant, toothache plant**

This is an easy annual to grow in any sunny garden. Seeds or started plants are generally available at the garden center or online.

References

1. Survival Medicine Blog. 2014. *When there is no dentist Indian toothache plant to the rescue.* https://survivalmedicineblog.com/2014/11/07/when-there-is-no-dentist-indian-toothache-plant-to-the-rescue/
2. Paulraj, J et. al. 2013. *The genus Spilanthes, ethnopharmacology, phytochemistry, and pharmacological properties: a review.* Advances in Pharmcological Sciences

It's A Gas

Back in the "old days of gardening," by which I mean before about 1985, most reference books about perennials were published in England. In this country information was found mostly in the form of catalogs from respected seed and plant suppliers. In 1970s and 1980s America, the production and use of perennial garden plants was in its infancy.

So there I was, newly excited about growing perennials, with the catalogs encouraging me to try all sorts of wonderful introductions. One I was particularly intrigued with was something called gas plant. I recall reading that plants emitted a flammable gas that one could ignite! And the catalog photos were beautiful.

Gas plant happily growing in Montreal

"In hot weather, old flowers or seed pods emit a flammable oil which, on a windless summer evening, can be ignited with a match resulting in a brief vapor burn."[1] Personally, I didn't really believe a word of it, but that is how the common name came to be.

Wherever I lived, I tried to grow them. They perished quickly in Montreal, Michigan was no better, and Georgia was too hot. Plants died relatively quickly but during their short life spans I became a pyromaniac. I went through entire matchbooks trying to light the suckers, but all I had to show were crispy leaves and burned fingertips.

Although I have never been able to light up the night with gas plant fires, there are some wonderful displays online of others' successes.[2] So it must be true!

By the way, if you can grow this plant it is quite stunning, fire stories aside. Where I see them in the UK, the West Coast, and other suitable locales, they are beautiful. A lemony fragrance is released when the foliage is rubbed or crushed.

The Plant

Dictamnus albus   **Gas plant**

Gas plant is relatively easy to grow where conditions are to its liking. It is said to be hardy to USDA zone 3, and since I have seen it growing in the Montreal Botanical Garden, that may well be true. No doubt, they are far more likely to do well in the North than the South.

Well-drained soils and full sun are musts. As fine a learning experience as they are, don't spend your child's college funds on them.

References

1.Missouri Botanical Garden. *Dictamnus albus.* http://www.missouribotanicalgarden. org/PlantFinder/PlantFinderDetails.aspx?kempercode=c490
2. Gas plant: the plant you can light on fire, 2011. https://www.youtube.com/ watch?v=pQTZyS7BKV8

False Indigo -
Americana In The Garden

False indigo is truly part of Americana. When I speak to audiences, I often ask a few questions I call "American Horticulture Quiz 101." The first question is, "What was the first subsidized agricultural crop in the United States?" Inevitably, shouts of corn, tobacco, cotton, and hemp ring out, none of which is correct.

Yellow flowers of B. tinctoria

It turns out that in the 1700s the British Empire's demand for blue dye far outstripped its ability to process it. This is because most blue dye came from the indigo plant, *Indigofera*, native to the West Indies. There was simply too little of it to satisfy the demand.

The English remembered the rather worthless colonies across the ocean, and soon botanists discovered that roots and flowers of the native baptisia, (*B. australis*) could be processed into a blue dye. Its quality was not as high as real indigo, so it quickly became known as false indigo.

In 1747, the first shipment of indigo left for England, and within two decades more than a million pounds would be shipped each year, making the dye one of the colony's largest exports, second only to rice. These two crops were excellent companions because rice could be grown in the swampy lowlands while indigo

False indigo in a Pennsylvania garden

could be grown on higher ground. Indigo production was an extremely labor-intensive, multiday process that was profitable only when it was done on a large scale with slave labor, which limited its production to plantations. The production of indigo caused a spike in the importation of African slaves—who would eventually outnumber whites in the colony by two to one—while lining the pockets of the colony's elite[1].

False indigo was grown for only a short period; true indigo was soon farmed and harvested. However, *Baptisia* opened the indigo markets from the colonies to England.

The original dye was actually made from the leaves of this species and the yellow-flowered *B. tinctoria*. Indigo was referred to as "the blue gold of the South," with Charleston, South Carolina as its growing and shipping hub. Over time, all species of *Baptisia* became known as false indigo.

OF NAKED LADIES AND FORGET-ME-NOTS

Baptisia spp.   *False indigo*

Few plants are as rewarding as false indigo. Not only do you have a wonderful story to tell garden visitors but it is also a long-lived, easy-to-grow plant for the sunny garden. Blue forms are the most common, but plants bearing yellow or white flowers are easy to find and equally handsome. Interestingly, the least common of the false indigos in gardens today is *B. tinctoria*; it simply is not as good a garden plant as other species and hybrids available to gardeners.

'Purple Smoke' hybrid false indigo

A good deal of hybridization has resulted in selections with a diversity of flower color and plant height. Low maintenance and high value make this a plant for every garden and landscape. I enjoy the variable colors and sizes, and would not be without at least one false indigo in my garden. Plants are cold hardy to USDA zone 4.

References

1. Growing indigo in South Carolina. Historical insights
http://www.ancestry.com/historicalinsights/indigo-south-carolina

Medicinal Bugleweed

This amazing groundcover seems to be in almost everyone's garden. Plants are equal opportunists, blanketing gardens from north to south with handsome foliage and colorful lavender-blue flowers. People often use the genus name *Ajuga* as the common name but the derivation of that name is obscure.

The emergence of the term bugleweed is equally mysterious. Some suggest it was derived from "bugulus," a thin pipe used in embroidery—the flower's thin corolla is thought to resemble it. Early writers also speak of the plant as "abija," "ajuga," "abuga," and "bugula," and the common English name, bugle, is clearly a corruption of one or another of these forms.[1]

Bugleweed in flower

Regardless of the etymology of the name, plants were thought to heal all sorts of ailments and drive away various diseases. One of the early herbalists, Nicholas Culpeper, wrote that "an ointment made with the leaves of Bugle, Scabious and Sanicle bruised and boiled in hog's lard until the herbs be dry and then strained into a pot for such occasions as shall require, it is so efficacious for all sorts of hurts in the body that none should be without it."[2] Scabious is a common name for pincushion flower (*Scabiosa*) and sanicle is a common name for the British herb *Sanicula*.

The Plant

Ajuga reptans   ***Bugleweed***

This is one of the easiest plants to establish in the garden. Generally it is recommended for shady areas, although in the North plants tolerate full sun. Many cultivars are available.

Be a little cautious; they are effective spreaders and may outgrow the area you wish to cover. They're frequently found growing into grassy verges past the garden's edge. Some people call this phenomenon "buglelawn."[3] Plants are cold hardy to USDA zone 3.

'Burgundy Glow' bugleweed

References

1. Grieve, M. 1931. *A Modern Herbal*, Harcourt, Brace & Co
2. Culpeper, N. 1653. *The complete herbal*. W. Foulsham & Co, London, UK
3. Armitage, Allan M. 2008. *Herbaceous Perennial Plants – a treatise on their identification culture and garden attributes*. 3rd ed. 1109 p. Stipes Publishing, Champagne, IL

Butter And Eggs, Anyone?

Growing up in Canada, we would see these snapdragon-like plants along the roadside and in meadows. I did not realize it was a European native, which, over time, has become an invasive species in many areas of North America. We simply called it butter and eggs.

Butter and eggs

The common name is pretty simple to understand, as the flower is pale yellow, with a bright orange lip, making the color and shape similar to butter and eggs.

The other common name, toadflax, may have originated from the resemblance of the mouth of the flower to the wide mouth of a toad. The toad reference may also have come from the botanist William Coles who believed that toads sometimes sheltered themselves among its stems.[1] The foliage of young plants resembles flax (*Linum*), accounting for the latter part of its name.

Many uses were historically ascribed to toadflax; in particular, it was thought to be useful to relieve the itch and pain of insect bites. Poultices made from the foliage of yellow toadflax were used to relieve the bites from the swarms of flies that tormented settlers in New England.

The most common use of yellow toadflax was as a dye. For centuries it had been used in Germany to make a yellow dye, and immigrants, especially the Mennonites, were delighted to find the herb already established in the New World. Soon they were cultivating it in fields to color their homespun apparel and other items. Once dyes were commercially manufactured, fields were abandoned, thus accounting for its success as an invasive species today.

The Plant

Linaria vulgaris   ***Butter and eggs***

While rather pretty, this plant does not really belong in gardens. They produce thousands of seeds that result in way too much butter and far too many eggs for one garden. However, they are attractive to pollinators. Flowers are pollinated by large insects, including bees, that can force themselves into the snapdragon-like blooms.

References

1. Coles, William, 1656. *The art of sampling, or an introduction to the knowledge and gathering of plants.* 123 p. London, UK

Forget-Me-Not!

There are so many stories about the forget-me-not that I could write a separate book about this one plant. However, here are three tales of how this little blue flower got its name.

I have always been bewitched by the story of the two lovers separated by a fast-moving river. The young man was determined to cross the river to be with his lady. He leapt in and swam as hard as he could but the current was too strong. As he finally reached the other bank, he desperately grabbed some flowers growing there, but they came away in his grasp. He clutched the small blue flowers in his hand and as the river carried him away, he shouted, "Forget me not!" That is my story and I'm sticking to it.

The blue and yellow flowers of forget-me-nots

A similar tale arose in fifteenth century Germany in which a knight picked some blue flowers by the banks of a river for his love. In doing so, he fell in. As he was being swept away, he threw the flowers to her and cried out, "Forget me not."

Last, it is said that when the Lord had finished naming all the plants, a small one cried out, "Forget me not, O Lord!" and He did not.

Through medieval times these flowers were worn by ladies to show their faithfulness and enduring love. Forget-me-nots have also been associated with a number of groups. Alaska adopted the forget-me-not as its state flower in 1917.

Forget-me-nots brightening a shady path

In the Second World War, the Freemasons of Europe chose the forget-me-not as a symbol of their work. This provided an outward means of identification while lessening the risk of possible recognition in public by the Nazis, who were engaged in wholesale confiscation of all Masonic Lodge properties.[1]

The Plant

Myosotis	*Forget-me-nots*

These are wonderful self-sowers particularly useful in moist areas. They make lovely ground covers over time, and in cool areas, they can grow rampantly. In hot climates, they may not be particularly persistent. This plant is easy to grow from seed or transplants.

References

1. Alexander, 2009. *The story behind forget me not emblem.* Masonic network blog, Dec 11

The Resilient Fireweed

Some seeds need heat to germinate and indeed, fire often is the catalyst. The name fireweed comes from this plant's ability to rapidly colonize burned-out areas. It inhabits open areas, such as forest clearings and wildfire sites, with little competition.

As long as there is clear space and plenty of light, plants thrive and flower, but as the canopy fills in, they begin to die. Seeds remain viable in the soil for many years, and germinate if a new fire or other disturbance opens up the ground to the sun again. Fireweed was one of the first plants to appear after the eruption of Mount St. Helens in 1980.

Fireweed flowers in July in Alaska

Known in Great Britain as rosebay willowherb due to its resemblance to rose flowers and bay leaves, plants quickly colonized burned ground after the bombing of London in World War II. Another descriptive common name, for the same reasons, is bombweed.

Fireweed is the official floral emblem of the Yukon Territory in Canada.

The Plant

Chamerion angustifolium   ***Fireweed***

Plants used to be classified as *Epilobium angustifolium* but have recently been reclassified. The place to see fireweed is in open meadows in the North, where their pink, and occasionally white, flowers can cover entire acres. This truly beautiful and ecologically important species is not easy to establish in gardens. Plants are cold hardy to USDA zone 2, but seldom thrive in the East in areas warmer than zone 5.

It's A Dog's Life

Dogbane is a common roadside and meadow weed that's seldom recognized by gardeners. Its genus name is *Apocynum*, from the Greek meaning "poisonous to dogs." I think that is a pretty obvious reason for its common name. All parts of the plant are poisonous; I can find no reasons why dogs were specifically picked on.

Dogbane

The native plant usually referred to as dogbane is *A. cannabinum*, referring to the similarity of the plant to *Cannabis*, which was used as a fiber plant. In fact, dogbane was used by Indians to make rope, and is also known as Indian hemp.

The Plant

Apocynum cannabinum	*Dogbane*

Plants can be found in areas where soils are disturbed. They often flourish by the side of the road and are a common denizen of car junkyards. Long live dogbane for helping to cover up such eyesores.

How The Poppy Became
The Flower Of Remembrance

John McCrae was born in 1872 in Guelph, Ontario. Over the years he became a successful poet, physician, artist, and author. He served as a pathologist at Montreal General and Royal Victoria Hospitals, and later as head physician at the Royal Alexandria Hospital. He started writing poetry as a student and published approximately 30 poems in his life.

He served in the Boer War (1899–1902) and quickly became disillusioned about the cost of war in human and animal lives. Upon his return to Canada, he continued his medical studies at McGill University.

John McCrae, about 1914

Because Canada was part of the British Commonwealth, when England declared war on Germany at the outset of WWI, Canada immediately followed. Dr. McCrae offered his services as a doctor and artillery officer, and sailed for Europe in late 1914.

There is no such thing as a good war, but the atrocities of World War I were far beyond any previous conflicts. Constant artillery fire, endless mud, filthy trenches, and incredible stress were everyday events. Working out of an eight-foot-square dugout, he did what he could for the wounded before being transported behind the front lines.

On May 2, 1915, his close friend Alexis Helmer was killed by a German shell. McCrae was distraught. The next day, as he looked over a makeshift cemetery near Flanders, Belgium, he noted wild red poppies blooming among simple wooden crosses. He wrote a poem.[1]

It is not exactly known how the poem made its way to England but "In Flanders Fields" was published anonymously by *Punch* magazine in December 1915. It instantly struck a chord in anyone who read it and became a rallying post for events such as fund-raising and patriotic rallies. It was published in America in *Ladies Home Journal* in November 1918.

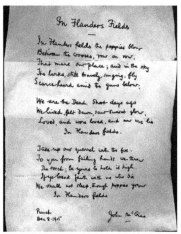

An autographed copy of In Flanders Fields. Unlike the printed copies widely distributed, McCrae's handwritten version ends the first line with "grow".[2]

John McCrae's words live on; unfortunately he did not. Dr John McCrae succumbed to pneumonia in Boulogne, France on January 28, 1918[1]

In Flanders Fields
John McCrae

In Flanders fields the poppies blow
Between the crosses, row on row,
That mark our place; and in the sky
The larks, still bravely singing, fly
Scarce heard amid the guns below.

We are the Dead. Short days ago
We lived, felt dawn, saw sunset glow,
Loved and were loved, and now we lie
In Flanders fields.

Take up our quarrel with the foe:
To you from failing hands we throw
The torch; be yours to hold it high.
If ye break faith with us who die
We shall not sleep, though poppies grow
In Flanders fields.

The Poppy Lady

As inspirational and beautiful a poem as John McCrae wrote, it likely would have faded into poetry books if not for an amazing young woman from a small town in Georgia.

Moina Michael was a schoolteacher in Winder, Georgia, who went on to lecture at the University of Georgia. In 1918, she was working in the YMCA Overseas War Secretaries' headquarters during its annual conference in New York. She came across the poem in *Ladies Home Journal* and was transfixed. She believed that a symbol was needed to commemorate the fallen soldiers. Because of McCrae's poem, she campaigned tirelessly that the red poppy be the flower of remembrance. She became known as "The Poppy Lady."[3]

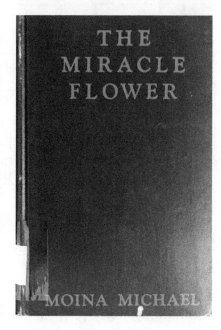

As a result of Moina's inspirational idea, the Flanders Fields poppy was first adopted as the flower of

The Flanders poppy

remembrance by the National American Legion on September 29, 1920. Remembrance Day, also known as Poppy Day, was first observed in England and Commonwealth nations on November 11, 1919. Within three years the poppy also became the symbol of remembrance, first in America, then quickly adopted in Canada, Britain, Australia and New Zealand. Other countries followed. Sales of paper poppies have raised millions of dollars for ex-servicemen and -women around the world.

Poppy field, Flanders, Belgium

If people should think that the poem by a medic and the work of a schoolteacher have been forgotten, this is not so. In 2014, the 100th anniversary of the start of "The War to End All Wars,"

OF NAKED LADIES AND FORGET-ME-NOTS

888,246 ceramic poppies were "planted" around the Tower of London, one for each British and colonial soldier killed during that war.[4] Such memorials continue to this day.

Few people know of Moina Michael today, but in 1941 she wrote a wonderful book, *The Miracle Flower, The Story of the Flanders Fields Memorial Poppy*. She also appeared on a U.S. three-cent stamp in 1949. Moina Michael died May 10, 1944, and is buried in Monroe, Georgia.[5]

The Weeping Window at The Black Watch Castle & Museum, Perth, Scotland, 2016

The Plant

Papaver rhoeas   **Flanders poppy**

The Flanders poppy is native to northern Europe and is readily found in meadows, fields, and disturbed soils. As a garden plant, it is best grown from seed sown in prepared soil during fall. Similarly, for a meadow component, sow seeds in full sun and flowers will appear the next spring. They can be seen on roadsides and in ditches in many parts of Canada and the United States.

References

1. Prescott, J.F. 1985. *In Flanders Fields: The story of John McCrae*, Boston Mills Press
2. McCrae, John, 1919. *In Flanders Fields and other poems*. Arcturis Publishing
3. *The Great War, 1914-1918, The story behind the remembrance poppy*
   http://www.greatwar.co.uk/article/remembrance-poppy.htm
4. The Guardian, December 14, 2014. *Blood-swept lands: the story behind the Tower of London poppies tribute*
5. Michael, Moina Belle, 1941. *The miracle flower*. Dorrance and Company, NY

Are They Really Called Hairy Balls?

To be a gardener, by definition, you must have a sense of humor. This is never more obvious than when looking at the fruit of this milkweed relative. Once you see them, the common name may not slip off your tongue in proper company, but nor will it soon be forgotten. Other more demure common names include balloon plant (for the inflated fruit), cotton bush (for the cottony fibers attached to the seeds when they disperse), and swan plant (fruit sort of look like swans).

Gomphocarpus physocarpus   *Hairy balls, swan flower*

Plants are considered annuals in most parts of the country. They grow 4 to 6 feet in height and, except for the interesting fruit and guffaws they may elicit, they really are not particularly useful garden plants. They do attract butterflies but are even more attractive to aphids. They also can reseed rather aggressively.

The plant was recently reclassified to this genus; it used to be *Asclepias physocarpa*.

Fruit of hairy balls

All Those Bursting Hearts

I am not sure if the common name, hearts-a-bursting, is sad because of love lost, or exuberant because of love overflowing. Either way, you may agree it's appropriate when you see the fruit of this native plant. The name comes from the fruit, which, when it opens, looks like a bursting heart. It is rather difficult to actually describe what this heart might look like and words do not do it justice. It must be seen to be understood.

It is sometimes called strawberry plant based on the fruit color.

The Plant

Euonymus americanus   *Hearts-a-bursting, strawberry plant*

The deciduous shrub is usually found in woodlands of the eastern United States and southern Canada. It is an underused garden plant, perhaps because it is rather forgettable until the fruit start to form. At that time, it comes into its own and you can talk about love, unrequited or fulfilled. Not only can you tell stories about it, it is quite ornamental as well.

Partial shade and moisture are prerequisites for good growth.

Fruit of hearts-a-bursting

Those Indestructible Hens And Chicks

Hens and chicks belong to the genus *Sempervivum* which means "live forever." If treated right, that is what they will do. Plants were considered to be so indestructible that they were often planted on thatched roofs to help with the integrity of the roof and to slow down fire.

'Clothilde'

Plants grow by rosettes (without stems). The common name comes from the large central rosettes (hens) and the subsequent smaller rosettes around it (chicks). Another common name is cats and kittens.

Sempervivum   **Hens and chicks**

I love these plants: they are resilient, they are handsome, and they are cute. However, mostly they are tough. For best success put them in the worst soil and the sunniest, driest exposure you have. The only warning I have about growing them is that drainage must be good; they do poorly in wet soils.

'Pacific Sparkler'

In ideal conditions, they will thrive. However, if you baby them, you will baby them to a quick death. They are hardy at least to USDA zone 4.

Dozens of weird and wonderful cultivars are available, from deep green to deep purple, from plain Jane to plants that look like they are covered with cobwebs.

Cobweb hens and chicks

Stay Away From Hogweed

I came across hogweed, actually giant hogweed, in a friend's garden in Denver, Colorado. It was impossible not to admire the 12-foot-tall plants with such incredibly large, white, umbrella-like flowers. They were like Queen Anne's lace on steroids. However, we both knew to stay away for two good reasons. First, it was, and is, a federally listed noxious weed. We knew about the invasiveness but it was for the second reason we wanted to avoid them. This stuff is dangerous! Even mild contact with its sap results in painful blisters and burns, making poison ivy seem like a joy.

Hogweed, about 8 feet tall

Some excellent references can be found that describe the plant, compare other species closely related to it, let people know what to do if they see it, and of course, display gruesome photos of the damage it can inflict.[1, 2]

However, nowhere could I find a respectable reference as to the name hogweed. The only reason I can find is that while most animals avoid it, hogs and pigs eat it.

The Plant

Heracleum mantegazzianum   *Hogweed*

Hogweed is likely to be found more in the northern and central states than in the South. If you come across it, stay away. It can be confused with Queen Anne's lace (*Daucus*), false Queen Anne's lace (*Ammi*), and wild parsnip (*Pastinaca sativa*). They are closely related and have similar flower forms. The most obvious differences are in height and size of stems; hogweed is significantly larger in all aspects than the other three. Wild parsnip, which also causes skin reactions, has yellow rather than white flowers.

References

1. New York State Department of Environmental Conservation. *Giant hogweed*. http://www.dec.ny.gov/animals/39809.html
2. Pearson, M. 2015. *Great, something else to worry about: giant hogweed*. CNN. http://www.cnn.com/2015/08/04/us/giant-hogweed-feat/

What Does The Hollyhock Have To Do With Holly?

Who would come up with a name like hollyhock? It has nothing to do with a holly plant, nor someone spitting in the gutter. In fact, it is a name that seems to belong in the "no one has any idea" category.

Plants are native to China and were adopted as a symbol of the Tokugawa Shogunate during the Edo period (1603–1867). Wearing this emblem showed respect to the shogun. Harming a hollyhock was punishable by death.

Hollyhocks mix

Plants found their way to the Holy Land, and then to the British Isles, likely from the Crusaders returning from the Holy Wars. In Wales, the plants were called "Hocys Bengaida,"(*hoo' kiss ben gade' a*) for "holy mallow" plant, because it came from the Holy Land. It is thought that the current name is derived from "holy-hoke" in reference to the Welsh name. Hollyhocks are beloved by many because of the beautiful flowers and the ease of growth in many parts of the world. In fact, the hollyhock is the official flower of the Taos, New Mexico garden club.

The Plant

Alcea   *Hollyhock*

These are usually quite tall plants (often 5 feet or more) that do best in cool climates and full sun. They have been bred extensively so that many quite wonderful colors are available. Unfortunately, they are susceptible to rust fungus and are particularly attractive to Japanese beetles. Plants are cold hardy about to USDA zone 4.

'Indian Spring'

Purple Flowers At
The Homestead

A number of celebrities are so well known that they need only one name. In sports, LeBron, Ali, Renaldo, or Tiger bring instant recognition. And celebrities like Cher, Madonna, Bono, Elvis, and Oprah need no further details beyond their first names. In our extremely small world of gardeners and landscapers, very few plants can make that claim. Perhaps the Wave Series of petunias or the SunPatiens® name stand alone, and they likely have interesting stories behind them.

As to a specific plant, one-namers are even fewer. Maybe 'Annabelle' or 'Endless Summer', but such examples are few and far between.

However, I am always asked to tell the story of 'Homestead Purple'. It may not be as recognizable as Elvis or LeBron, but it is known to almost anyone in the plant business and to many gardeners.

Way back in the late 1980s, two young plantsmen were driving down the road in a little red pickup. Both loved horticulture, and were always talking about woodies and herbaceous plants they enjoyed. It was a cold March day in north Georgia as they passed a patch of purple beside a house a few hundred yards off the highway. Without warning, the little red truck made a U-turn and the boys slowly started down the long dirt drive.

The purple patch was magnetic but the dwelling was not. It was a place you drove by, not to. With dead cars in the front, an assortment of debris on the porch, and the entire place looking a little down in the mouth, it brought strains of "Dueling Banjos" to their minds.

The good-looking fellow put his friend in front and they cautiously knocked on the door. A teenaged boy, hair askew, shirt missing, and feet bare, emerged. When they asked him about the flowers, he turned around and yelled, "Mama, someone's here to see your flowers!" Soon, Mama appeared in her housecoat and curlers. When we told her we wanted to know more about the brilliant blossoms in the yard, she broke into a Cheshire cat-sized grin. It was probably the first time anyone had ever noticed her garden.

'Homestead Purple' verbena in England

The good-looking fellow, his friend, and Mama walked over to the purple patch. Soon they were joined by daughters, brothers, dogs, cats, and other assorted mammals. It was as if "Kumbaya" were going to break out around a campfire. No sooner had the good-looking one said, "That's a verbena," when he received a sharp elbow in the ribs. Mama looked at him as if he were illiterate and retorted, "That's not verbena, that be vervain."

Vervain is the old-fashioned name for verbena and she was, indeed, correct. A fine time was had by all, and when the boys asked if they could take some plant pieces, they walked away with seven cuttings in a plastic bag. In a few weeks, the cuttings were rooted and about to be planted outside. However, before they were to be seen by anyone, a name was needed.

The plant was named to commemorate the house from which it came, and called 'Homestead Purple'.

The good-looking fellow ran the Trial Gardens at the university and each year he introduced a number of new plants for the ornamental industry. If people in the industry wanted to try them, they were allowed to take a few cuttings back to their greenhouses. When growers and landscapers visited the gardens during the Open House that summer, they all wanted to try the new verbena.

Allan Armitage and Michael Dirr, friends and plantsmen

These were the days before plants were routinely patented. He simply asked that if they liked the plant enough to sell it, they use the name 'Homestead Purple'. And they did.

OF NAKED LADIES AND FORGET-ME-NOTS

Within two years, the variety had become a major item for landscapers and growers across the Southeast. In three years, it was in most greenhouses across the country. In five years, it was in England and other European countries, and soon became the standard by which other verbenas were compared. It was the first "mega" verbena not grown from seed, and the genus took off as breeders throughout the world offered new plants to their customers.

As beautiful as the dozens of newer introductions released since are, 'Homestead Purple' is still offered right alongside. Even after more than 20 years, it is like the little engine that could—it simply will not go away. Every time one of the daughters of the good-looking fellow sees the plant, she says, "That could have been my children's tuition."

Who were these two young men who brought this fine plant to us? Allan Armitage and Michael Dirr.

The Plant

'Homestead Purple' Verbena

Plants are easily grown in most well-drained soils in a sunny location. While it was introduced as an annual, plants usually return yearly in zones warmer than USDA zone 7. Removing spent blooms during summer results in additional flowers. If plants become spindly, cut them back to the ground; they will return in a few weeks with even more vigor.

The Curious Tale Of
The Horny Goat Weed

I happened to be in an organic food store and found myself confronting rows of bottles and vials of herbal medicines. I noticed tablets of Echinacea, comfrey, Ginkgo, St. John's wort, saw palmetto, and there in bold letters, was a bottle labeled "horny goat weed." Really, I can't make this stuff up.

It turns out the name was not concocted in a smoke-filled back room by dirty old men but rather by Japanese goat farmers. They noted that in fields where epimedium grew and leafed out

The resemblance of the flower to the bishop's mitre provides the common name bishop's hat

OF NAKED LADIES AND FORGET-ME-NOTS

in spring, the males (billy goats) were far more randy and the incidence of "goatlets" (kids) exploded. As I studied the bottle a bit more intently, it was obvious that even with all the blue pills and bathtub ads on TV, men still use these over-the-counter supplements for sexual performance. And why not, really—how can thousands of billy goats be wrong? The active ingredient in epimedium is icariin, the same as in the blue pills.

'Rose Queen' barrenwort

Barrenwort is the most popular common name for *Epimedium*. It was believed that the leaves of the alpine form (*E. alpinum*), if ground up and added to wine, would prevent conception for five days if drank after menstruation. In 1597, it was given the English name of 'Barren Woort' by Gerard[1]. . . because, as some authors affirme, being drunke it is an enimie to conception." For more information on "worts", see Doctrine of Signatures.

Bishop's hat is also used to describe epimedium flowers because some species bear flowers that resemble the mitre of a bishop.

The Plant

Epimedium   *Horny goat weed, barrenwort, bishop's hat*

Epimedium is one of the finest perennials for dry shade. If you have a shady area that is difficult to irrigate, barrenwort is the number one choice. When I remember to do so, I remove all foliage in early spring; that way, the flowers are more visible.

Dozens of species and hybrids await, some evergreen, some deciduous. They all have striking flowers in spring, often rose or yellow, and attractive foliage the rest of the season.

References

1. Gerard, John, 1597. *The Herball or Generall Historie of Plantes*. Imprinted London, UK, John Norton

Epimedium x versicolor 'Sulphureum'

There Is No Ice In The Ice Plant

There are many plants that go under the ice plant moniker. In California, ice plants are usually *Mesembryanthemum* and *Lampranthus*; in South Africa, *Carpobrotus* is an ice plant; and the same name is given to *Disphyma* in New Zealand. The most common ice plant in American landscapes and gardens is *Delosperma*.

These plants must have something in common if the same name is used for all of them. In fact, there are many parallels: they belong to the same family and their colorful daisylike flowers and succulent leaves are also comparable. To the untrained eye, they are similar enough to all be called ice plant.

'Jewel of the Desert' ice plant

Ice plant is not called an ice plant because it is cold hardy, but rather because the flowers and leaves seem to shimmer as though covered in frost or ice crystals. Some botanists claim such shimmering occurs because the foliage is covered with transparent flakes that resemble tiny pieces of ice. However, according to researchers at New Mexico State University, the common name is in reference to bladderlike hairs on the leaf surface that reflect and refract light in a manner to make it appear that they sparkle like ice crystals.[1]

The Plant

Delosperma	Ice plant

Ice plants are excellent for poor soils and dry areas. They tolerate drought well, and can be used successfully in rock gardens and borders in the garden. Hybridization has resulted in some beautiful new selections such as 'John Proffitt' and 'Jewel of the Desert'. Ice plants have become popular landscape choices in the last five years.

Ice plant is cold hardy to USDA zone 7.

References

1. Smith, C., April 9, 2015. *Ice plant.* New Mexico State University http://aces.nmsu.edu/ces/yard/2005/040905.html

Can A Plant Really Be Impatient?

The common name and the genus name of *Impatiens* are the same, which is not uncommon. After all, we call plants in the *Hydrangea* genus hydrangeas, and genera such as *Viburnum*, *Anemone*, and *Aster* are familiar as common names as well.

Unlike the others, impatiens has a story to tell—actually one to show.

If you come across a planting of impatiens, particularly in fall, look closely for seedpods. Tenderly pluck the fruit away from the plant and gently hold it between thumb and forefinger. Give it a tiny squeeze, and the seeds will violently explode. Once you have the hang of it, do the same for friends and kids. Tell them not to squeeze, but within 10 seconds someone will, and with shrieks of surprise, then pleasure, so will everyone else. That is why they are called impatiens, and why their other common name, touch-me-not, is so appropriate.

Bedding impatiens flowers

One year, on the first day of class, I placed ripe seedpods on each student's desk but said little about them. I simply suggested they might not want to touch them. Within the same ten-second time frame, kids were jumping away from the irascible seeds, and cries of surprise coursed thorough the classroom. They never forgot where impatiens got its name. In the United Kingdom and Commonwealth countries, they are also known as busy lizzies.

Impatiens seedpods

Impatiens walleriana   **Impatiens, touch-me-not**

There are hundreds of species of impatiens, including our native jewelweed, so named because of the shiny flowers, and New Guinea impatiens, for the area where they were first discovered.

The little seed bombs are most often found on garden impatiens, *I. walleriana*. They are for sale in every plant and grocery store in the spring. Unfortunately, most garden impatiens today are hybrids and are often sterile, so the job of finding those impatient seedpods has become more difficult. However, if vigilant, you will find some. If fertile hybrids are allowed to reseed, the resulting plants will be much closer to the wild forms and seeds should form readily.

A native impatiens, common around streams and rills, is known as jewelweed (*I. capensis*). These always produce seedpods and may be better subjects, should you come across them while hiking.

Plant impatiens in a location receiving afternoon shade. I prefer planting them in containers to avoid some of the disease problems associated with these plants.

Preaching With Jack

Jack-in-the-pulpit is but one of a dozen common names given to this plant, but it is surely the most widely used. The name "Jack" refers to the erect stalk (spadix) enveloped by the shroud (spathe), like a preacher standing in a pulpit. Some people prefer parson-in-the-pulpit, seeing a country parson elevated over his congregation. Lord and lady is also used as a common name, referring to the ostentatious spadix wrapped in the rather flamboyant royal purple spathe.

Jack is well hidden beneath the pulpit

These names all make some sense, but one that does not is Indian turnip. Supposedly Native American tribes prepared the corms as a starchy food, like one would a turnip. The problem with this story is that the entire plant contains high levels of calcium oxalate—biting into the corm would be like biting into shards of glass, not only rather uncomfortable but also poisonous. Even after thinly slicing and boiling for at least 12 hours, slivers of calcium oxalate remain.

There were many more fruits and berries around that would have been far more efficient food sources than this. The name still exists but the idea that this very toxic and debilitating plant would be used for food is poppycock. Green Deane, the well-known forager and writer, has done extensive research on ways to prepare Jack for eating.[1] His bottom line: don't eat it.

The Plant

Arisaema triphyllum   *Jack-in-the-pulpit,*
                                 parson-in-the-pulpit, Indian turnip

The Jacks arise from a small corm and are, without doubt, one of the more engaging woodland species in spring. They may either be male (smaller, shorter, and with no fruit) or female (taller, larger, with bright red berries). They will change gender on their own if conditions are to their liking. Plant in shade, water in well, and enjoy these wonderful native ephemerals.

References

1. Deane, Green, Eat The Weeds Blog. *Arisaema triphyllum: Jack and Jill and no hill.* http://www.eattheweeds.com/arisaema-triphyllum-jack-and-jill-and-no-hill-2

The Story Of The Maltese Cross

The Maltese cross is a symbol associated with the Sovereign Hospitalier Order of John of Jerusalem of Rhodes and of Malta, a Catholic religious order founded about 1099. The order's name was later simplified to the Order of Malta.

The cross is an eight-pointed white cross having the form of four "V"-shaped elements, each joining the others at its vertex, leaving the other two tips spread outward symmetrically.

The Maltese Cross

The flower represented (*Lychnis*) has five, bright red petals, each notched, to make ten rather than eight points. However, the shape of the flower was sufficiently similar for it to be given the name Maltese cross.

Maltese cross

The Plant

Lychnis chalcedonica   *Maltese cross*

A stunning red is the most common flower color, though other hues are available. Plants grow to 18 inches tall and bear handsome dark green foliage. Place in full sun and soil with excellent drainage.

Maltese cross is cold hardy to USDA zone 4. Plants are better subjects for Northern gardens, as they do not tolerate hot temperatures well.

Salmon form of Maltese cross

Where the Longhorn Cattle Feed On The Lowly Jimson Weed

Plants have always played an important role in the history of any country, usually in the form of food and fiber. Even in this small book, I have mentioned the importance of potatoes, indigo, and carrots, and how a poppy plant has been stitched into our history.

Jimsonweed (*Datura*) occupies a different niche in American history. The native origin of *Datura* is in question but is believed to be from Mexico and became naturalized in much of North America. It is also known as thorn apple (for its thorny round fruit), trumpet weed (for its trumpetlike flowers), and under more sinister names like devil's breath, devil's weed, and hell's bells. Sources argue as to its exact native origin, but there is little doubt it grew on our shores as early as the 1500s. And, as it turns out, it grew near Jamestown, Virginia, in such numbers it became known as Jamestown weed.

Handsome flowers of jimsonweed

As the plant spread across the country, it became known as jimsonweed.

The hallucinogenic properties of Jamestown weed were well known to the natives of the area, and to the colonists as well. Ingesting any part, but certainly the seeds, results in significant behavior changes, essentially driving one mad (another well-known name is locoweed).

Early times in Jamestown saw numerous conflicts involving the colonists, Indians, and the British. The Indians and colonists were fighting over the same land while the British were constantly trying to manage the unruly colonists. One such uprising was led in 1676 by Nathaniel Bacon, a well-to-do colonist opposed to the British governor William Berkeley. Although the causes and ramifications of Bacon's Rebellion are but a footnote in history, one of the accounts of the uprising mentions Jamestown weed specifically.

The soldiers were tricked into eating food secretly laced with Devil's Breath shortly before they were due to fight. The result was that they spent "several days making monkey faces and generally acting like lunatics."[1]

One soldier was found "stark naked, sitting in a corner like a monkey, grimacing at his comrades. In such a frantic condition they were confined, lest they should, in their folly, destroy themselves—for they would have wallowed in their own excrement, if they had not been prevented. And then after 11 days returned themselves again, not remembering anything that had passed."[1]

Even today, truly crazy people still experiment with jimsonweed, with very unpleasant results. One less-than-enlightened user became thus enlightened. "To sum it up in one word . . . insanity. That's what it feels like if you start to snap out of it and realize what's happening, but then you just go back into this state of total confusion and it's enough to drive anyone crazy. I have

The name "thorn apple" comes from the fruit

no motivation to do it again anytime soon, maybe someday years from now just for some crazy fun. But this *Datura* seems to be something not of this world. The hallucinations were accompanied by delirium and confusion that made them seem real. This stuff truly is the devil's weed."[2]

The plant certainty has its devilish references, but for many, it's more often recognized as the signature song of one of America's most revered singing cowboys—Gene Autry. "Back in the Saddle Again" was released in 1939, and was associated with Autry throughout his career. It was subsequently recorded by several other artists, including Slim Whitman, and in 2001 was voted as one of the top 100 Western songs of all time.

"I'm back in the saddle again,
Out where a friend is a friend.
Where the longhorn cattle feed
On the lowly jimson weed,
Back in the saddle again.

I'm riding the range once more,
Totin' my old 44.
Where you sleep out every night
And the only law is right,
Back in the saddle again."[3]

Datura stramonium   *Jimsonweed*

The white, sometimes purple trumpets make a beautiful show in late spring and early summer. Place in full sun and water well. Plants are annuals and seldom reseed.

Poisonous plants have always held fascination for gardeners, but planting these in your garden is like having a swimming pool with no fence—trouble just waiting to happen.

References

1. Berkeley, Robert, 1705. *The history and prefent state of Virginia, in four parts.* London, UK
2. Erowid Experience Vaults Blog. *Truly the Devil's Weed.* https://www.erowid.org/experiences/exp.php?ID=16996
3. Autry, Gene and Whitley, Ray. 1939. *Back in the saddle again*

The Fable Of Johnny Jump Up

Johnny jump up is but one of many names for the three-colored wild violet. The name refers to the habit of the seeds exploding from the flower, resulting in "plants jumping up" everywhere. Many species of violets do this (which is why so many are obnoxious weeds) but only this particular one earned the nickname. Why the name Johnny, I am not sure.

This plant pops up in literature as often as in the garden. Here is a part of the poem *How Spring Comes to Shasta Jim* by Henry Van Dyke, from 1913.[1]

She's loopin' down the hillside—the driffs is fadin' out.
She's runnin' down the river—d'ye see them risin' trout?
She's loafin' down the canyon—the squaw-bed's growin' blue,
An' the teeny Johnny-jump-ups is jest a-peekin' thru.

Johnny jump ups

Heartsease is another name often seen for this plant. Two reasons for the name are provided. The first from its use as an herbal supplement as a palliative for many maladies. Using it puts one's heart at ease.

The second is that it may have acquired this name because it was used in love potions and charms. I like this reason best.

By the way, "Johnny Jump Up" is also an Irish drinking song from County Cork and refers to a strong cider, made more potent by being stored in whiskey barrels. Who knew?

The Plant

Viola tricolor   *Johnny jump up, heartsease*

Plants that require no investment, no labor, and no maintenance are few and far between. Violas include garden pansies and many other weedlike violets; this one is simply a breath of fresh air. Plant a few in a sunny spot on a path between stones or anywhere they can have free rein. They are only 3 to 6 inches tall, so they will never become an eyesore. The cheerful sunny flowers will soon be enthusiastically jumping up all over the place.

References

1. *The Poems of Henry van Dyke*, 1921. C. Scribner & Sons

Who Is Kissing Whom Over That Gate?

A plant called kiss-me-over-the-garden-gate is worth having in the garden for the name alone. If any name should be accompanied by some good yarns it should be this one, but even considering the oddities of other common names, this one seems to make little sense.

The label may have arisen because these unruly plants are 6 to 8 feet tall. That in itself is not distinctive but during the summer, the long drooping flowers arch over the stems. In anyone's garden, the bright rose-red flowers can easily dangle over the garden fence or a gate. Perhaps the name makes sense after all.

Regardless, what fun it is to have such a lovely name in the garden.

The Plant

Persicaria orientalis   **Kiss-me-over-the-garden-gate**

This is a pass-along plant, one best passed over that garden gate to friends. It can be quite aggressive, in some areas moving towards invasive. For most people, it is an annual, but can often reseed, sometimes with abandon. Be careful.

However, it is quite beautiful and has many fans, including birds and butterflies. Plant in full sun. A garden gate is a useful addition.

Kiss-me-over-the-garden-gate, close up of flowers

Alchemy And The Lady's Mantle

Some say that the "lady" in lady's mantle refers to the Virgin Mary, with whom the plant was associated in the Middle Ages. The leaf was thought to resemble a coat or mantle, thus the name "lady's mantle" was born.

It is difficult to determine the accuracy of such a story, and while I suppose it makes sense, I wonder why that particular name stuck with gardeners. The more sensible common name for this plant is "dewdrops" because of the drops of water formed on the edge of the leaves.

Actual drops of dew in the morning

Western alchemy is described as the science with the goal of changing ordinary metals into gold. It was further defined as a means to find a universal cure for disease, or the "elixir of life." Even respected scientists such as Isaac Newton and Robert Boyle were interested in a recipe for the Philosopher's Stone, a legendary substance that could turn iron and lead into gold.[1] If some of the greatest scientists who ever lived were dedicated alchemists, who are we to dismiss alchemy as "witchcraft?"

I mention this story because a number of reports suggest that alchemists believed the drops of water seen on the edges of the leaves were the purest water on earth, even claiming it to be "heaven's water," and the key to producing the legendary Philosopher's Stone.[1]

Believe what you wish, but the name dewdrops certainly seems a far more intuitive common name for this most interesting plant.

Lady's mantle in spring

The Plant

Alchemilla mollis   **Lady's mantle, dewdrops**

I love this plant for the front of the garden, along a path, or as an informal planting anywhere afternoon shade is available. Plants do not tolerate hot summers particularly well, so they are more common in the North than the South. Fabulous chartreuse flowers cover the plants in spring.

References

1. Bosveld, Jane, 2010. *Issac Newton, world's most famous scientist.* Discover Magazine, July-August

Love In The Mist

There seems to be lots of love and heartbreak going on in the garden, what with love-in-a-puff, bleeding hearts, hearts-a-bursting, and love-lies-bleeding. Finding the origins of love-in-a-mist involves maidens, emperors, and a good deal of imagination.

The "mist" likely refers to the threadlike leaves of the plant. The "love," on the other hand, is anyone's guess. It likely refers to the flowers within the "misty" leaves, but Harold Roth[1] suggests that the name comes from the legend about Emperor Frederick I (1125–1190). Apparently, when he was on the way to the Crusades, a water spirit seduced him with promises of love. While in this somewhat hypnotic state, he was drowned in the hip-deep water by the spirit. This plant sprang up at the shore and displayed the water spirit's hair. Those who believed this story felt that the flower looked like lips surrounded by hair, thus the "love in the mist."

Love-in-a-mist, the plant

Black cumin is a spice derived from a close cousin of this plant, *N. sativa*. Its medicinal properties are heralded. In fact, according to legend, it cures "everything but death."[2]

OF NAKED LADIES AND FORGET-ME-NOTS

The Plant

Nigella damascena   *Love-in-a-mist*

This is one of the easiest annuals to grow in the garden. Seed is readily available. Plant in full sun and let them roam through and about other plants in the garden. Love-in-a-mist is one of the more popular choices for the English cottage garden look. The flowers are pretty but the striped pod is the most handsome part of all. The fruit can be used in dried arrangements with great success.

Dried pods of love-in-a-mist

References

1. Alchemy Works Blog. *Nigella damascena, love-in-a-mist.* http://www.alchemy-works.com/nigella_damascena.html
2. Ji, Sayer, 2013. *16 more reasons black seed is "the remedy for everything but death".* http://www.greenmedinfo.com/blog/16-more-reasons-black-seed-remedy-everything-death2. Green Med Info, Nov 29

Sniff And You Shall Sneeze

Sneezing is a common human condition, and people sneeze in many different ways. From loud, trumpetlike blasts to mousy squeaks, this response to irritants is as common as coughing in the movie theatre.

Sneezing is, essentially, a nerve transmission that tells your brain something is in your nose and needs to come out. Pollens, irritants, dander, even looking at the sun may cause one to sneeze. Dozens of compounds can make us sneeze—in fact, recipes for sneezing powder are all over the internet. However, there is little history as to why many plants were saddled with names related to sneezing.

'The Pearl' sneezewort

Apparently in the case of sneezewort, the pungent smell of the foliage induces sneezing. This is likely why the plant was conferred its specific epithet *ptarmica*, which comes from the Greek *ptarmikē*, for a plant that causes sneezing. The "wort" aspect of the common name refers to its ability or usefulness, thus "makes one sneeze."

The dried leaves were also historically used to make a sneezing powder at a time when sneezing was thought to be useful to rid the body of bad humors.

Recently the plant gained significant notoriety when young Harry Potter read about the Befuddlement Draught, in which sneezewort was an important ingredient. It was kept with other potion ingredients in the Potions Classroom at Hogwarts School of Witchcraft and Wizardry.[1]

The Plant

Achillea ptarmica   **Sneezewort**

Plants are native to Europe and grow best in cool climates. I do not recommend them further south than zone 6. However, the handsome buttonlike white flowers are excellent for border plants and the flowers can be cut and enjoyed, fresh or dried. It's hardy to USDA zone 3.

Many choices are available; the most common is 'The Pearl'. Plant in full sun in well-drained soils.

References

1. Rowling, J.K., 2003. *Harry Potter and the Order of the Phoenix*, Scholastic Inc

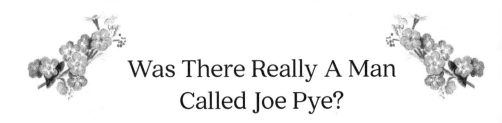

Was There Really A Man Called Joe Pye?

Many botanical names carry a person's name (*Jeffersonia, Achillea, Lewisia*) but few common names bear people's names. Was there really someone called Joe Pye, and is a plant really named for him? There was and there is.

Joseph Pye was a Mohegan Indian and an herbalist who lived in the late 1700s near Stockbridge, Massachusetts. One of the herbs Joseph recommended was *Eupatorium purpureum*, plentiful in the area, for the treatment of typhoid fever.

Joe Pye weed behind crocosmia and sedge

One of the first mentions of Joe Pye's weed was provided by a Mohegan writer, Samson Occom, who in July, 1787 ". . . went to Joseph Pye, alias Shauqueathquat, and had very agreeable conversation with him."[1]

OF NAKED LADIES AND FORGET-ME-NOTS

Joseph's plant induced sweating, and was useful in the treatment of a number of ailments. The first printed reference to the common name appeared in Amos Eaton's *Manual of Botany* (1818), in which he referred to the plant as "joe-pye (from the name of an Indian)."[2] Its medicinal use became more accepted in the third edition (1822) when Eaton mentioned that President Zephaniah Swift Moore, the second president of Williams College in western Massachusetts, "ascribed his recovery from a very alarming fever to the liberal and continued use of a tea made with these plants."

'Little Joe' Joe Pye weed

So yes, there was such a person as Joe Pye and *Eupatorium* became known as Joe Pye's weed, shortened to the common name used today. One of the finest accounts of Joseph's interaction with this plant was written by Richard Pearce.[3]

By the way, *Eupatorium* has officially been changed to *Eutrochium*. Joe Pye weed is now *Eutrochium* purpureum.

The Plant

Eutrochium purpureum   *Joe Pye weed*

These have always been revered as meadow plants or subjects for native plant installations. In open spaces, they are magnificent but often too tall for smaller suburban gardens. However some shorter nativars have been developed ('Little Joe', 'Little Red') which are excellent for the garden. Plant in full sun but place behind shorter plants; even the dwarf ones are at least 3 feet tall. They flower in late summer and fall.

References

1. Brooks, J. 2006. *The collected writings of Samson Occom, Mohegan: leadership and literature in eighteenth-century Native America*, Oxford University Press US

2. Eaton, A. 1918. *A manual of botany for the northern and middle states, 2nd ed.* Websters & Skinners Publishing

3. Pearce, R., Nov, 2010. *Joe Pye – the Name Behind the Legend.* PrairieWorks Blog. http://www.prairieworksinc.com/2010/11/15/joe-pye-the-name-behind-the-legend/

Love Lies Bleeding

Between kiss-me-over-the-garden-gate, love-in-a-mist, naked ladies, and horny goat weed, there seems to be a lot of "nicky-nacky" going on the plant world. On the other hand, there is no lack of despair either, given hearts-a-bursting and bleeding hearts. And to add to the misery, along comes love-lies-bleeding.

This annual probably gets its unusual name from the color (heart red) of the dozens of dangling tassel-like (as if bleeding) flower stems. It is also sometimes called kiss-me-over-the-garden-gate, but that name is usually associated with *Persicaria* (which see).

Some of the diversity of love-lies-bleeding

Amaranthus caudatus   **Love-lies-bleeding**

This is a tough plant, growing well in poor soils and in hot, sunny locales. It does not tolerate a lot of nutrition nor does it tolerate "wet feet."

Plants can reseed with vigor. However, they are shallowly rooted and can be easily pulled if they become too numerous. One packet of seed will provide remarkable diversity in resulting plants.

The Bane of Wolves,
The Hoods of Monks - Same Plant

Whenever I see a healthy stand of these plants, I always want to look at the flowers closely and check out their hoods. The flowers are unique because of the large upper sepal overlapping the rest of the flower, like a hood. I did not know many monks growing up, so I can only assume that what they wear is similarly shaped.

Perhaps naming the flowers for the hood of a monk does make sense

The common name likely arose during medieval times, because of the obvious similarities between an aconitum flower and a monk's hood.

Plants are also highly toxic. In Europe, arrows were tipped with an extract made mainly from the roots, and bait was laced with it. It was used as a poison for many predators but mostly was the bane of wolves.

Flowers of monkshood and lion's tail in a New York garden

OF NAKED LADIES AND FORGET-ME-NOTS

The Plant

Aconitum   *Monkshood, wolfsbane*

Plants are grown from tubers, like potatoes. They prefer cool summers and cold winters, and do not perform well in areas warmer than USDA zone 6. Plants generally flower in late summer or fall, providing a valuable asset for fall color.

For obvious reasons, they should not be sited where curious children or pets might discover them.

Picking On Mothers-In-Law

Someone definitely has it in for mothers-in-law. I know of no father-in-law nor brother- or sister-in-law plant. At least in my limited opinion (I have only one mother-in-law), many have been tarred with the harshness of a few.

The sharp leaves must have reminded someone of a mother-in-law's sharp tongue and the name stuck. Sad, unfair—but occasionally true.

Perhaps the other common name, snake plant, based on its long leaves, is a little kinder to members of one's family.

Another abuser of mothers-in-law is the mother-in-law cushion, a wicked-looking, painfully spiny, barrel cactus, *Echinocactus grusonii*. Must have been a bad day at the in-laws for whoever named this.

Mother-in-law cushion

The Plant

Sansevieria trifasciata   *Mother-in-law tongue, snake plant*

Certainly, this is one of the easiest houseplants to grow; it is almost indestructible. Plants need little light, moisture, or fertilizer to maintain a regal posture in the home. Numerous cultivars are available, and all are excellent.

Mother-in-law plant, handsome and sharp

The Story Of The Naked Ladies

I am too old to be shocked by much anymore, but as I roam around plants and gardens, it seems to me that there must have been a club of good old boys smoking something that resulted in some rather bawdy names.

For example, one fine September afternoon, a friend and I came upon some beautiful red flowers blooming at the top of naked stems. Absolutely no leaves—just bare stalks.

I said, "Look at those beautiful resurrection lilies." That name seemed appropriate to the way the stalk and flowers rose from ground like a beautiful Phoenix. With a twinkle in her eye my friend looked at me and said, "You mean the naked ladies?"

The nude plants we were looking at were *Lycoris*, and she explained that naked ladies was once a common name for many bulbs, it stuck with this one. How could I argue—the stem was as bare as a baby's bottom, and I simply can't imagine those boys in the back room calling them naked men.

Naked ladies strutting their stuff in early fall

By the way, a third common name for the bulb is naked boys, but that doesn't work nearly as well either.

The Plant

Lycoris radiata   *Naked ladies, resurrection lily*

Bulbs are best planted in fall. Dig a large hole approximately 3 times deeper than the bulb is wide. For an impressive show, plant at least 6 bulbs, approximately 6 to 8 inches apart, and fill in the soil about halfway. Water in well, and then fill in the rest of the hole with soil. Additional fertilizer is not needed at the time of planting.

Long narrow leaves will emerge in spring and should be fertilized about a week after with a complete fertilizer (e.g. 10-10-10, liquid formulation). After 3 to 4 weeks, the leaves start to yellow and will totally disappear by early summer. Some people like to mark the position of the bulbs in the garden so they don't plant anything over them. In September to October—when you least expect it—naked ladies miraculously appear. They persist for only about two weeks, but what a wonderful show they make.

Plant in full sun and provide adequate drainage so bulbs are not sitting in standing water at any time.

Hallelujah, It Is Risen!

You are standing in front of a large oak tree covered in crusty growths. If you do not know what you are looking at, you would bet that the oak tree has some awful disease all over it. Upon closer inspection, however, you might note that the brown patches are shriveled ferns, and bet number two would be that they are well and truly dead. You'd lose that bet too. Stay out of Vegas!

Shriveled plants of resurrection fern

This remarkable fern has adapted ways to stay alive even during periods of prolonged drought. It is estimated that resurrection ferns lose about 75 percent of their water during dry conditions. They can lose up to 97 percent of their water in extreme droughts and still "come back from the dead" when rains reappear.[1] As a comparison, most plants perish if they lose 10 percent of their moisture.

Another plant that appears to be come back to life is the resurrection lily, *Lycoris* (which see).

The Plant

Pleopeltis polypodioides   *Resurrection fern*

This is not a "garden" plant in the common sense of the word. It is an epiphyte, meaning it takes moisture and nutrients from the air, while being anchored to another plant, often an oak tree. It is not parasitic. Plants are found throughout the Southeast, as far north as New York, and west to Texas.

References

1. National Wildlife Federation. Resurrection fern
http://www.nwf.org/Wildlife/Wildlife-Library/Plants/Resurrection-Fern.aspx

Resurrected plants on a white oak

Who Could Make Money Selling Sweet Potatoes?

This book contains only three instances in which I feel a specific cultivar is sufficiently well known to stand on its own in a gardening conversation: 'Homestead Purple' verbena, 'Annabelle' hydrangea, and 'Margarita' sweet potato. I have no doubt there are dozens more, but those three quickly come to mind.

Today's gardens, landscapes, containers, and even window boxes overflow with ornamental sweet potatoes. Perhaps they are not as ubiquitous as hydrangeas or petunias, but they are certainly popular. The most amazing part of the ornamental sweet potato story is that nearly all the cultivars available today, and there are dozens, arose because of a single slide on a screen in Raleigh, North Carolina.

One of the first plantings at UGA Trial Gardens

The South has been blessed with amazing plantspeople. In the 1990s, they were introducing new woody and herbaceous plants at a remarkable rate. The Southern Plant Conference, a biennial meeting of interested breeders, researchers, and industry members, started in Athens, Georgia, in 1989 with well over 200 people. By the time the show was held in Raleigh in 1995, nearly 600 people were in the audience.

Leaders in the study of woody ornamental plants, including Michael Dirr, Don Shadow, and Ted Stevens, among others, were discussing and displaying the future in hydrangeas, viburnums, dogwoods, crape myrtles, and cherries. Herbaceous plants were not big on the docket but I was scheduled to speak anyway. My screen filled with heliotrope, pentas, alternantheras, ruellias, and some perennials I had been working on. It was only when I put an image of a sweet potato on the screen did people question my sanity: a sweet potato? Who in their right mind could make money selling sweet potatoes?

Thank you, Hunter Stubbs

I had been running the Trial Gardens at the University of Georgia for some time and had been talking about new plants and how they performed in the heat and humidity. In the late 1980s and through the 1990s, there was tremendous interest by breeders and industry people to expand the list of plants that were heat and humidity tolerant. More people were moving southward, huge markets in the South were opening up, and often plants bred in England, Holland, or the Pacific Northwest were simply not suited for the climate.

In 1994, I received a piece of a purple-leaved sweet potato from my colleague Dr. Butch Feree. He claimed that it was rescued from a dumpster by a volunteer at the Sweet Potato Research Center in Chase, Louisiana. Apparently the tubers were of poor quality and it, among hundreds of other taxa, was culled from the program. I looked at the thing, shrugged my shoulders, and proceeded to root it and then plant it in the Trial Gardens. Oh my, how it grew! It was quite beautiful. My colleague suggested it be called 'Blackie' and that is the plant I showed in Raleigh the next year.

When I showed this sweet potato as a possible new ornamental plant, people in the audience snickered—politely of course; after all, we were in the South. Regardless of my prognostication that this could be an excellent plant for growers and landscapers, it was forgotten as the next slide appeared. That would likely have been the end of the story if not for an amazing young graduate student at North Carolina State University by the name of Hunter Stubbs. He approached me as I was leaving and said. "I can't believe you are talking about a sweet potato as a landscape plant, but if you are interested, I have one you might want to try." He handed me a sad-looking plant with two chartreuse leaves in a four-inch pot. I thanked him even though neither of us believed it would amount to a hill of beans, and then I asked, "What do you want to call it?" Hunter called it 'Margarita' because of its chartreuse leaves.

I planted it in the garden that spring. Just like 'Blackie', it flowed; from containers, from baskets, and as a groundcover. The combination of the two sweet potatoes was quite fantastic and when

Who needs maple leaves when 'Margarita' leaves are available? Meet granddaughter Kate.

industry people visited the trial gardens that summer, they couldn't believe the vigor and beauty of 'Margarita'.

Similar to my other new plants in the Garden (see the story of 'Homestead Purple' verbena), growers could take cuttings and sell them under the name I had given. Within five years, it was all over America. Today, you can't help tripping over it everywhere you go.

Its success spurred research and breeding into other cultivars and today, a dozen or more choices are available from respected breeders. Yet 'Margarita' is still one of the most popular sweet potato out there, likely because it was not patented and anyone can grow and propagate it. Who would have thought that dumpster diving in Louisiana would result in one of the most recognized plants in ornamental horticulture?

The Plant

Ipomoea batatas   ***'Margarita' sweet potato***

Place in containers or in the garden in full sun. Plants need a good deal of water to become established, but other than that, they are easy to grow. Their vigor makes it hard to combine them with slower-growing plants in mixed containers or baskets, but a plant that grows fast is a problem that many gardeners do not mind having.

In fact, my granddaughter Kate loves to frolic in 'Margarita' leaves in the fall as much as she does maple leaves.

Plants are annual and do not flower in the landscape.

Way Down Yonder In The Pawpaw Patch

Next time you play trivia, you can stump all you friends with this question, "What is the largest edible fruit indigenous to North America?" The answer: pawpaw.

The first documented mention of pawpaws was in 1541 by the Spanish explorer Hernando de Soto during his explorations of the southeastern United States. He claimed that Native Americans in the Mississippi valley region were cultivating them for food.[1]

It is most abundant in the Midwest and has another common name that I bet most people in Indianapolis, Muncie, and Richmond do not know. The large fruit bear some resemblance to a banana, and thus, Indiana Banana was coined.

Indiana banana makes some sense but where did "pawpaw" come from? The name is thought to have derived from the Spanish word *papaya*, the name given to the fruit of the papaya tree (*Carica papaya*). That plant is also known as papaw. The

Pawpaw fruits

fruits are superficially similar and the tropical pawpaw name may have been transferred to the North American pawpaw by the de Soto expedition.

The fruit is tasty to some but has also been described as an "unendurable insipidity."[2] George Washington planted pawpaws at his home in Mount Vernon, Virginia, and pawpaws were among the many plants that Thomas Jefferson cultivated at Monticello. Jefferson also shipped seeds to his friends in Europe.

They were invaluable to the members of the Lewis and Clark expedition. In 1806, the members of the expedition subsisted almost entirely on wild pawpaws for several days. "The party appear perfectly contented and tell us that they can live very well on the pawpaws."[3] Daniel Boone and Mark Twain were also reported to have been fans of the fruit.

The Plant

Asimina triloba   **Pawpaw, Indiana banana**

The pawpaw is a clumping understory tree, growing naturally in well-drained fertile soils. It multiplies by root suckering and large populations can result. Trees can reach heights of 25 to 30 feet.

Pawpaws are native to large areas of the United States and Canada, from the eastern seaboard, south to northern Florida, west to Nebraska, and north to southern Canada. It's cold hardy to USDA zone 5.

References

1. Hackluyt, R. 1609. *A narrative of the expedition of Hernando de Soto into Florida*. By a Gentleman of Elvas. Published at Evora 1557. Translated from the Portuguese by Richard Hackluyt. London
2. Thwaites, R. G. 1899. *The Jesuit Relations and Allied Documents. Travels and explorations of the Jesuit missionaries in New France 1610–1791*. Vol. LIX. Cleveland: The Burrows Brothers Publishers
3. Lewis, M. and W. Clark. 1806. *September 18, 1806, entry in The Journals of the Lewis and Clark Expedition*, ed. Gary Moulton. University of Nebraska Press. 2005

What Does Passion Flower Have
To Do With Passion?

It is hard to beat the beauty of a passion flower. All parts of the bloom including the filaments, stigmas, stamens, pistil, sepals, and petals, are obvious to the naked eye. But what does the flower have to do with passion?

It turns out that creativity was alive and well in the minds of early Catholic scholars. The passion refers to Christ's suffering and the flowers are a reminder. In the fifteenth and sixteenth centuries, Spanish missionaries adopted the unique physical structures of this plant, particularly the numbers of its various flower parts, as symbols of Jesus's last days, especially his crucifixion.

Passion flower (P. x belotii) in Athens, Georgia

The ten petals and sepals represented the ten true apostles (St. Peter and Judas Iscariot were not included); the filaments, which can number more than one hundred, represent the crown of thorns; the ovary, the Holy Grail; the three stigmas, the three nails; and the five anthers represented the five wounds.

There are dozens of species of passion vine but the one in the southern United States (*P. incarnata*) goes by the common name of maypop. Opinions as to where the name arose are many but it likely was an alteration of a Virginia Algonquin name "maracock," translated to maypop.

Passiflora   *Passion flower, maypop*

Vines climb with tendrils and are easy to train on arbors or allowed to run through shrubs. Many species and hybrids are available, some with large flowers, others much more diminutive. Place in full sun. Plants are annuals in most of the country.

Fruit of maypop

How Rose Campion Lit The Way

The genus *Lychnis* is said to be derived from the Greek word lychnōs, meaning lamp. This possibly refers to the ancient description penned by Greek physician and pharmacologist Dioscorides around 55 AD.[1] He suggested that the hairs on the woolly leaves could be used as lamp wicks. In fact, this was one of the first plants to be known as lamp flower, because its leaves were downy and soft, "fit to make candlewicks."[1]

The specific epithet *coronaria* is roughly translated as "pertaining to garlands." The blooms were said to be used as garlands for victors in public games or tournaments. Much of the older literature still refers to plants in the genus as "champions."

The name "campion" is derived from "champion," probably because of this practice. The name rose campion should probably be magenta campion but that is for another day.

Rose campion

OF NAKED LADIES AND FORGET-ME-NOTS

The Plant

Lychnis coronaria   **Rose campion, lamp flower**

One of the easiest plants to establish, rose campion needs little besides sun and good drainage. However, this gray-leaved plant with screaming magenta flowers may not be for everyone. The flowers almost glow, and some designers have difficulty coordinating them with other garden elements. Design-challenged as I am, I have no such dilemma.

Plants reseed but they are not invasive. Some excellent cultivars, such as 'Oculata', are much easier on the eyes. Plants are cold hardy to USDA zone 4.

References

1. Dioscorides, P. 1554. *De Materia Medica*

'Oculata' rose campion

Raising The Nap

Perhaps you have seen teasel on the side of the road, or in a meadow somewhere. I remember my first handling of the seed heads; they were bristly, they were tough, and they hurt when I touched them. I did not think of the plant much until my college days when girls started talking about teasing their hair. Maybe there was a connection.

It turns out that teasing hair is not much different than teasing wool, and this is where this lowly roadside weed gets interesting. Teasing wool was an important job in medieval England. In the wool trade, wool fiber is teased out, prior to the carding process, which disentangles and cleans the wool prior to spinning. The first "implements" for teasing and carding were the seed heads of *Dipsacus*, which became known as teasel. A card originally consisted of teasel heads set in a frame and was used to comb the cloth to make it soft and fluffy, a process known as "raising the nap."

Dipsacus sativus, Tatton

The hand carder had a dozen or so teasel heads in a frame but a larger version, called the teasel gig, was invented in the 16th century. Machines of teasel gigs were manufactured in the 19th century and consisted of over 3000 teasel heads to raise the nap.[1] In the mid 20th century, the teasels were replaced with metal teeth, called the Moser Raiser.[2]

Teasels for the woolen industry were historically grown in England and France but in 1826, Dr. John Snook, of Somerset, England moved to the town of Skaneateles, New York. He realized the fields around the town were excellent areas to cultivate teasel. He imported seed from Europe and by 1840, Skaneateles teasels became the nap raising standards of the United States

OF NAKED LADIES AND FORGET-ME-NOTS

woolen industry. It was estimated that the value of Skaneateles teasels shipped from the town during 1875 alone was $200,000, a lofty sum at that time.[3] Skaneateles became known as The Teasel Capital of the World. Teasels were replaced in the United States around 1950 with equipment using metal teeth.

Teasel

The Plant

Dipsacus   **Teasel**

Essentially these are weeds. Weeds with an interesting story, but seldom seen in a "garden." However, if you wish to raise a teasel field, simply provide full sun and moisture, and you will be raising nap with the best of them.

References

1. http://spinwheelspin.blogspot.co.uk/2011/08/national-wool-museum-in-wales-personal.html
2. The National Wool Museum. https://museum.wales/wool/about/
3. Maior, Jack. Have teasels, will travel. Major-smolinski.com. (http://major-smolinski.com/CNY/TEASELS.html.)

Was There Really
A Wandering Jew?

I have often wondered why this common plant is called wandering Jew. People constantly comment on its rampant growth, so I understand the "wandering" part, but why a Jew? Why not a Christian, or a Muslim, or why a religious connotation at all? There are dozens of plants that wander about our gardens, and how this particular one ended up as the wandering Jew, I did not know.

Was there a real Jew wandering around out there somewhere? In fact, there are many versions of such a person, even though arguments abound concerning basis in fact. Here is one I share with you, based on a story by Horace Scudder.[1]

The Wandering Jew *by Gustave Doré, 1856*

After being sentenced to death by Pontius Pilate, Jesus was made to carry his cross as he passed through Jerusalem. Many people watched, stood in doorways, or looked out their windows. One of these was a shoemaker named Ahasuerus. He knew that Christ would be dragged past his shop, and called his household to see this person, who, he said, had been deceiving the Jews.

Ahasuerus stood in his shop's doorway and perhaps wishing to curry favor with the crowd, roughly bade him go forward. Jesus looked at him, and obeyed. But as he moved away, he turned to the shoemaker and said, "I shall at last rest, but thou shalt go on till the last day."

'Purpurea'

On that day, Ahasuerus went to his house, but not to stay. He bade his wife and children farewell and began wandering. He wandered from Judea to Greece, from Greece to Rome. He grew old, and his face was like leather. He was never seen to laugh. He went through storms and the cold of winter, he endured the dry heat of summer, but no sickness overtook him. He joined armies that were going forth to battle, but death never came his way, though men fell by his side, and he forever wandered.

Now and then, learned men would draw him into talk, not knowing who he was, and would find him familiar with great events in history. It was not as if he had learned these in books. He talked as if he himself had been present.

Then the learned man would shake his head, and say to himself, "Poor man, he is mad," and only after the old wanderer had left would the thought suddenly come, "Why, that must have been the Wandering Jew."

Other people have their own opinions on such a story; another I enjoy reading is from a blog called Plants are the Strangest People.[2]

'Blue Sue'

| *Tradescantia* | *Wandering Jew* |

Plants definitely wander, but should not be considered invasive in the garden. In fact, they are handsome ground covers.

Plant in full sun or afternoon shade. They are easily propagated by vegetative cuttings. Consider them annuals in most of the country; however, they may come back as far north as USDA zone 7b. Plants are also used as houseplants, and tolerate low light indoors, although they may get quite leggy.

A number of excellent selections are available; the purple one ('Purpurea') is by far the most common. However I personally think 'Blue Sue' is prettier and a better performer.

References

1. Scudder, H.E, 1899. *The book of legends, told all over again.* Houghton Mifflin
2. Plants are the strangest people, 2008. *The wandering jew (Tradescantia zebrina).* http://plantsarethestrangestpeople.blogspot.com/2008/09/wandering-jew-tradescantia-zebrina.html

I'm Just A Pincushion - Do Everything She Says

The pincushion flower is aptly named. Simply hold a flower of any of the many types of *Scabiosa* species at eye level. Look across the top of it and you will notice all the "pins" sitting in the middle of the flower. The "pins" are actually the stamens, but isn't that a good name?

However just like the story of pinks (which see), few people younger than thirty will have a clue what a pincushion is. Unless, that is, they are familiar with the Texas blues and rock band ZZ Top. I must confess, I am not a fan, but the more I research plant names, the more I learn that even celebrities love them. Great songs about pokeweed, jimsonweed, and Johnny jump up have often appeared on bestseller charts. ZZ Top and gardening, who would have guessed?

'Kudo Pink'

I'm a pincushion, gotta face the facts
I'm just a pincushion, do everything she asks
I'm a pincushion, gotta face the facts
I'm just a pincushion, do everything she asks[1]

The other, more historic, name for plants of this species is "scabious." Its leaves were thought to relieve the itch of scabies and other afflictions of the skin, even sores caused by the Bubonic Plague. In his seventeenth century tome *The Complete Herbal*, Nicholas Culpeper wrote, "The green herb bruised and applied to any carbuncle or plague sore, is found by certain experience to dissolve and break it in three hours' space. The same decoction also drank, helps the pains and stitches in the side."[2]

The Plant

Scabiosa caucasica   **Pincushion flower**

This is an excellent perennial for gardeners almost anywhere. The typical color is purple to lavender but cultivars in whites and pinks may also be found. Plants grow to about 2½ feet in height and should be placed in full sun.

They bloom in late spring and early summer and make excellent cut flowers to bring into the house. Not only that, they attract hordes of bees and butterflies. Plants are cold hardy to USDA zone 5 and to zone 4 with protection.

While the species is still available, excellent selections in deep blue, pink, and white are available.

References

1. ZZ Top, 1994. *Pincusion*, from album Antenna. RCA Records
2. Culpeper, N. 1653. *The complete herbal*. W. Foulsham & Co, London, UK

What Does Candytuft Have To Do With Candy?

Candytuft is one of those early spring-flowering perennials that is almost foolproof. Perhaps its name comes from the handsome tuft of slightly fragrant white flowers that look like a candy treat. That is a good story, but as much as my grandkids might like it, it isn't so.

Perennial candytuft

The botanical name *Iberis* tells us that plants are native to Iberia, the European peninsula that includes Spain and Portugal, as well as Greece and the island of Crete. The ancient name for Crete was "Candia," and as the botanist John Parkinson wrote, "These doe grow in Spaine and Candie not farre from the Sea side."[1]

When it was imported to England during the reign of Queen Elizabeth, the term "candiatuft" became candytuft. That's not as much fun for the kids, but such is boring history.

The Plant

Iberis   *Candytuft*

Many species and cultivars are available to the gardener. One of the many annual species is rocket candytuft, *I. amara*. Plants are upright and flower in white or lavender.

The most popular form is perennial candytuft, *I. sempervirens*, usually flowering in white but also occurring in lavender. Most of the breeding has been done with this species. Plants are cold hardy to about USDA zone 3.

References

1. Parkinson, J. 1629. *Paradisi in sole Paradisus Terrestris*. London, UK.

Rocket candytuft

How Pinks Got Their Name

If you ever wore a boutonnière for your graduation dance, and your date was cheap, then you are acquainted with the carnation, the most familiar of all the pinks *(Dianthus)*. However, there are a ton of dianthus selections for the garden, used in beds, containers, and window boxes. Most gardeners know the common name is pinks and nearly all believe it came from the fact that most flowers are indeed pink. Not so fast!

Look at the petals on any dianthus, from cut flower carnations to miniature garden plants. Notice that every petal is serrated, as if cut by pinking shears! This is actually where the common name comes from.

'Festival' pinks. Note the serrated petals

I just thought that was the coolest thing ever, but as I told the story to one of my plant ID classes, then delivered the punch line, half of my students gave me blank looks. They nodded to each other as if the professor was doddering even more than usual.

Then I realized that hardly anyone under the age of 30 even knew what pinking shears were. The longer I taught, the higher the percentage of vacant gazes. So now when I tell the story,

I whip out my wife's old pair of pinking shears, cut a piece of paper, and fill in the details on why dianthus came to be known as pinks.

The Plant

Dianthus   **_Pinks_**

Dozens of different dianthus await the gardener, from 6-inch low growers to 3-foot-tall mini carnations. And they are certainly not all pink anymore; in the last 20 years breeders have created a rainbow of colors.

The shorter pinks may be placed in full sun at the front of the garden bed or at the edge of mixed containers. They are also excellent for window boxes. Taller ones comport well almost anywhere.

They tend to bloom in spring through early summer; spent flowers may be removed to encourage another wave of flowers. They are excellent in the South as companions for pansies, in the North as spring-planted, summer-flowering annuals and perennials. Nearly all pinks are pleasantly fragrant.

'Desert Cranberry' pinks

The Snapping Dragon

When I first considered writing this book, I was going to research only names that might have interesting stories and were relatively unknown. However, the more stories I share in my travels, the more I realize that what I may consider obvious may not be well known at all. And fun stories like that of the snapping dragon should never disappear.

Of course, the common name comes from the appearance of the flower—a little like a dragon—but the story is all about making it snap. If you have not snapped a dragon lately, simply put your hand behind the flower, and squeeze the "cheeks." The dragon will snap. Ask someone to put his or her finger inside the open dragon's mouth, then let it snap shut. Believe it or not, shrieks will ensue. If you are not sure how to do this, watch my video.[1]

Snapdragon: snapper form

Snapdragons: butterfly form

Antirrhinum majus *Snapdragon*

So many colors and heights of this popular annual are available that you can be sure to always have dragons to play with. They are at their best during cool times, and can tolerate frosts to about 25 degrees F. Plant in early spring in the North or in fall in the South and plants will flower for many months.

Some breeding has resulted in non-snapping snapdragons; they are referred to as butterfly types. They are excellent garden plants but not nearly as much fun.

References

1. Armitage, A. 2016. *Snapping snaps.* https://www.youtube.com/watch?v=4BiyRrF86Nk

Love In A Puff

I first was made aware of a vine with the twee name many years ago. I am not sure where I found it, but I soon planted it in my garden. The vine was somewhat disappointing; it was rather frail with forgettable, small white flowers. But I was curious about the common name; I thought, "The plant must do something to earn this nickname." And it does.

As the vine continues to grow, the flowers give way to *papier mâché*-like puffy fruit. They are well camouflaged. If you don't look carefully, you might miss them. That explains the puff but the love was still a mystery.

Fruits of love-in-a-puff

The fruit will dry out and turn brown during the season. Once they're dry, open them and look at the seeds within. This is where storytelling gets to be fun. Pluck out the 2 or 3 brown seeds and show them off, one by one. Each seed will bear a white marking, often perfectly heart shaped. People will ooh and aah, and you have discovered the love in the puff.

Seeds of love-in-a puff

Plants have been used medicinally for a wide range of ailments including digestive disorders, rheumatism, and snakebites.

The Plant

Cardiospermum halicacabum   *Love-in-a-puff*

This vine won't win any prizes for showmanship or color, but on the other hand, it is one of the ten sacred flowers of the Kerala state in India[1], and it is easy to grow almost anywhere. It is most comfortable growing through shrubs or into other vines, like clematis or roses.

They are annuals and may reseed, but they will never be termed invasive. Saving the seeds and planting out the next spring allows love to remain in your garden for many years.

References

1. Dasa Pushpen (Ten Scared Flowers).
https://deepakrishna.wordpress.com/2010/08/10/dasa-pushpam-ten-sacred-flowers/

What Does
The Fox Say?

Many people know that *Digitalis* is the source of a powerful medicine digoxin, used for the treatment of heart issues. The medicinal properties of digitalis were first discovered in 1785.[1]

There are numerous species of foxglove. The most common, *D. purpurea*, is native to temperate Europe. The word "digitalis" means fingerlike. They were called finger flowers because "they are like unto the fingers of a glove, the ends cut off."[2]

Common foxglove

Thus, part of the common name makes great sense, but people have been debating why "fox" is associated with "glove." The earliest known form of the word is the Anglo-Saxon "foxes glofa" (the glove of the fox). Some people believe that the original name was "folksglove," referring to a glove of the "good folk" or fairies.[3] Their favorite haunts were the deep hollows and woody dells where the foxglove is common. The term "folksglove" was mentioned in a list of plants in the time of Edward III (1327–1377).[3]

Unfortunately, no single account is accepted by etymologists. In fact, it is pretty darn serious to these folks. The title of the article "Etymologists at War with a Flower"[4] aptly describes the passion of the debate.

Regardless, stories abound. One that is rather appealing paints the aforementioned fairies as out for no good. They gave the blossoms to the fox that he might put them on his toes to soften his tread when he prowled among the roosts.

> *Once upon a time, many years ago, there was a red fox who was always looking for ways to catch a chicken in Farmer Brown's chicken coop. Each time he would try, the chickens would hear him and began making loud cackling sounds. Immediately Farmer Brown would come outdoors with his shotgun ready to shoot any animal that approached his birds. The fox was so discouraged. He wanted to steal a chicken. His mouth would water every time he would think of eating one. One day as the fox was lying in the grass moping about his lack of opportunity in catching a chicken, a mischievous fairy approached him asking, "What's the matter with you?"*

> *The fox replied, "I want to catch a chicken but the chickens keep hearing me and making so much noise that Farmer Brown comes running to see what is disturbing them."*

> *The fairy smiled and said, "I know of a way to help you catch those chickens without them hearing*

you. Do you see that plant in the garden? It is called Digitalis. Remove four of the blossoms and put them on your feet. Wear them the next time you want to catch a chicken."

That evening when darkness arrived, the fox put the four blossoms on his feet and crept carefully and quietly to the chicken coop. He slipped inside and stole a chicken. He ran all the way home to his den without any of the chickens making any sound.[5]

White flowers of 'Emerson' in a Georgia garden

When all is said and done, there appears to be no explanation as to why foxes were given the glove. A leading etymologist simply believes the "fox" part was started by children as a game, and has nothing to do with a fox at all. He says, "In sum, foxglove means foxglove," and that it is just fine to "accept an etymology that is obvious."[3]

That explanation makes the most sense to me, and I am sticking to it.

The Plant

Digitalis *Foxglove*

Common foxglove, *D. purpurea*, is always easily available. Plants are biennial, meaning a winter dormant period is necessary before flowers form the next season.

Buy well-developed started plants in fall and place them in a sunny area of the garden. Many cultivars are available, and they are all handsome.

Plants are cold hardy to about USDA zone 5.

References

1. Withering, William, 1785. *An account of the foxglove and some of its medical uses with practical remarks on dropsy and other diseases.* London, UK
2. Parkinson, J. 1629. *Paradisi in sole Paradisus Terrestris.* London, UK
3. Grieve, M. 1931. A Modern Herbal, Harcourt, Brace & Co
4. Liberman, A. 2010. *Etymologists at war with a flower: foxglove.* Oxford University Press.
5. Garden Beauty, 2011. *A fairy tale of the fox and a fairy.* http://mghighlandgarden.blogspot.com/2011/05/fairy-tale-of-foxglove-and-fairy.html

Queen Anne, The Tatting Queen

If there is such a thing as a "correct" common name for Queen Anne's lace, it is likely wild carrot, a name first published by William Turner in 1548.[1] This makes sense as, botanically, it is close to an edible carrot; that is, their taproots are carrotlike. So why don't we call it by its correct name?

A number of plant names are related to needlework. Names such as pincushion flower and pinks can directly be linked to sewing accessories, as can Queen Anne's lace. Making lace by hand (think of collars and doilies) is referred to as "tatting." It is likely that many people today have no idea how lace is made; this art form is in severe need of "tatters."

In the early 1700s, tatting was immensely popular. Queen Anne of England reigned from 1702 until her death in 1714. Hers was not an easy life. It is hard not to feel sorry for someone who was constantly ill and who became pregnant 17 times but who died without any surviving children. However, she was well known for her skill at tatting, which was renowned and matched by few of her subjects.

Queen Anne's lace on a Pennsylvania roadside

It is said that she once pricked her finger while tatting and a small drop of blood fell on the lace. If you look closely at the middle of a Queen Anne's lace blossom, you will often see a purple flower in the center surrounded by lacework.

An equally, and perhaps more obvious explanation of the name, is that the purple flower represents the Queen, and the white flowers represent her lace collar. Many other explanations of the name may be found, with most having to do with the importance of the Tatting Queen.

Note the small purple flower on top

Daucus carota ssp. carota   ***Queen Anne's lace, wild carrot***

This "weed" escaped from Europe and is far more common as a roadside plant than in a garden. It is a biennial, meaning it lives only two years but reseeds with abandon. Thus, it never seems to go away. It has long roots—in fact it is truly a wild carrot. The roots even smell like carrots.

A variety of this plant, var. *sativa*, is the progenitor of the garden vegetable. If garden carrots were not picked and if they survived winter, their flowers the following year would look similar to those of Queen Anne's lace.

Not all flower heads have the obvious purple flower in the center; be sure to choose one that does when telling this story.

References

1. Turner, William. 1548 The Names of Herbes. Published for the English Dialect Society, Ludgate Hill

The Sweet Smell Of Sweet Woodruff

Quite a few flowers bear the sweet nickname, such as sweet flag, sweet bay, and sweet William. The "sweet" part of this common name is simple enough. The leaves of *Galium odoratum* smell like new-mown hay when dried and crushed. They are used in perfumery, not only on account of their own fragrance, but also for their property of fixing other scents. Plants are also used to disguise disagreeable odors.

The "woodruff" name is a bit of a puzzler, perhaps originating in the Middle Ages. The name appears in the thirteenth century as "wuderove," and later as "wood-rove;" the rove being derived, perhaps, from the French *rovelle*, a wheel, in allusion to the spoke-like arrangement of the leaves in whorls.[1]

This plant is also referred to as bedstraw because of the sweet aroma, but it is a closely related species, *G. verum*, whose common name is lady's bedstraw. The name is derived from its use in former days, even by ladies of rank, for bed stuffing. The fragrant scent is coumarin, which also helps kill fleas.

Sweet woodruff in a Canadian garden

The Plant

Galium	*Sweet woodruff, bedstraw*

Sweet woodruff has handsome white flowers on 6- to 8-inch-tall plants. They grow rapidly and can be used as ground covers. Plants perform best in partially shaded areas. However, they may perform too well in some gardens, particularly in the Midwest and farther north. Reports of aggressive weeds that smother other plants do not endear this as a "sweet" plant. It used to be known as *Asperula odorata*.

Both species are native to Europe, which helps to explain their popularity there. This is becoming naturalized in the northern states and Canada and may become an invasive weed.

Both species are cold hardy to USDA zone 4.

References

1. Grieve, M. 1931. *A Modern Herbal*, Harcourt, Brace & Co

The Curious Tale Of Sleepy Dick

Some common names just seem to fit, and even though you often can't repeat them, they make you chuckle. Not just smile, but an audible giggle when you think about the plant.

I have grown *Ornithogalum umbellatum* for many years; in fact, it was a common bulb in my old garden, and in many areas of the country. Although only 6 to 9 inches tall, plants proudly showed off starlike white flowers atop the foliage. I knew it as star of Bethlehem, and it was always handsome when in bloom.

However, the flower stems had a rather annoying habit of not standing straight and the flowers did not open until midmorning or even later. Pesky perhaps, but nothing I thought much about. Then one morning I was scanning a garden publication from the 1920s in which my lazy old plant was called sleepy Dick!

The gestalt was just a little much, and with apologies to all the fellows named Dick, I began to chuckle. And while I occasionally mentioned both common names to my close friends, I was not able to do so with my students in my class. I likely would have been taken to task by a well-meaning Southern Baptist.

Sleepy Dicks growing through iris leaves

If it were called sleepy Sam or sleepy Fred, it would have been easier, but not quite the same. Regardless of which common name you use, it is a beautiful and popular plant for the garden.

The Plant

Ornithogalum umbellatum   ***Sleepy Dick,***
                                           star of Bethlehem

Bulbs are best planted in fall. Dig a large hole approximately 4 inches deep. These are small bulbs; plant at least 15 of them, almost bulb to bulb. Fill in the soil halfway. Water in well, and then fill in the rest of the hole. Additional fertilizer is not needed at the time of planting.

Plants emerge in spring, flower for weeks, and then eventually go dormant in summer. The buds have an obvious green stripe on the outside. Flowers open to pure white on the inside.

The drawback to these bulbs is that, in some areas, they can become a major nuisance, growing into larger and larger clumps over time. In my garden I eventually had to dig, separate, replant some, and give others away. Be cautious.

Plant in a location in full sun or afternoon shade.

Sneezeweed Does Not Make You Sneeze

The common name of this plant made me think nervously of hay fever, symptoms of which have plagued me since I was a kid. Was this just another ragweed? I was wrong. Ragweed pollen is airborne, and afflicts many of us with hay fever symptoms, including sneezing. However, the pollen of sneezeweed is carried by insects and bees; it is not windborne. Thus it has nothing to do with hay fever, although it flowers about the same time as ragweed.

'Moerheim Beauty'

Alas, it was still saddled with the suggestive name—perhaps by the Menominee Indians of Wisconsin—who called it *aiatci'a ni'tcîkûn* meaning, "sneezing spasmodically."[1]

Apparently, the name was based on the historic use of the crushed dried leaves and flower heads to make a form of snuff that caused sneezing. In certain cultures and times, sneezing was regarded as a desirable way to rid the body of evil spirits or a way to loosen up a head cold. Falsely accused of being a sneeze plant, the name has stuck nevertheless.

Another common name for the plant is Helen flower, which makes a bit more sense. *Helenium* comes from the Greek word *hělěnion*, for the goddess Helen, who in Greek mythology was considered to be the most beautiful woman in the world. According to legend, she was married to King Menelaus of Sparta but was abducted by Paris, the son of the king of Troy. The folklore is not clear about whether she was abducted by or actually seduced Paris. Regardless, thus started the Battle of Troy.

'Mardi Gras'

It took ten years but finally with the clever use of a wooden horse the walls of Troy fell and the war ended. Myth suggests that Menelaus vowed to punish his wife in front of his people. Helen was brought to her husband, and, falling to her knees, tore her clothes to reveal her breasts and begged for her life, weeping the tears that became known as Helen's flowers.[2]

The Plant

Helenium autumnale   **Sneezeweed**

These perennials flower late summer into fall and are available in many colors and sizes. Full sun is best. Older cultivars tend to be 4 to 6 feet tall and include 'Moerheim Beauty', beautiful but big. Newer selections are much improved, growing only about 2 feet tall. A popular cultivar is 'Mardi Gras'. These may be used in gardens and containers without staking (unlike older cultivars). It's hardy to USDA zone 4.

References

1. Smith, H.H. 1924. Ethnobiology of the Menomini, http://www.manataka.org/page73.html
2. Trull, S. Common sneezeweed. US Forest Service. https://www.fs.fed.us/wildflowers/plant-of-the-week/helenium_autumnale_autumnale.shtml

How A Tuber Changed
The World: The Potato
And Ireland

These days, visiting Ireland is a joy. Wonderful gardens, friendly people, and remarkable history are to be found everywhere. It was not always like that.

Life was difficult in Ireland in the 1600s. All decisions of law were handed down from the English parliament; Irish rule was essentially nonexistent. This was nothing new. As early as 1307, the English crown decreed the Statutes of Kilkenny. These banned Irish dress, Irish customs, and Irish sport, even to the point that a person riding a horse on anything other than an English saddle could be jailed. No Irish could enter a chapel, church, or cathedral in his homeland unless an Englishman was present. Speaking Gaelic, or using Irish names, resulted in forfeiture of land and property to the king.

As would be expected, the Irish rebelled, the English retaliated, and on and on. To suppress the insurgency, Oliver Cromwell laid siege to the country in the mid-1600s. After the massacre at the Siege of Drogheda in 1641 and other atrocities, the Act of Settlement was passed, upon which Cromwell's supporters seized half of all the arable land in Ireland, about 8 million acres. Any Irish landowner who complained was sentenced to a life of bondage or evicted from the country altogether.[1]

The Penal Laws, enacted at the end of the seventeenth century, made conditions even worse. They essentially outlawed the Catholic religion; thus a Catholic could never sit on a jury, vote, buy land, practice law, attend school, serve an apprenticeship, possess weapons, or hold any government office. The Gaelic language was banned.[1]

Export trade was forbidden as Irish commerce and industry were deliberately destroyed. "In Ireland, people were to be forever illiterate, forever poor, and forever powerless."[1]

By 1835 half the rural families in Ireland were living in single-room, windowless mud cabins under unspeakable conditions. They lived in small communal clusters, with up to a dozen persons crammed into one hovel. In some cases, the shanties' occupants were actually the dispossessed descendants of Irish estate owners. It was not uncommon for a beggar in Ireland to mention that he was in fact the descendant of an ancient Irish king.

Land was taken by the English, and divided and re-divided into smaller and smaller tracts, so that Irish farmers could raise only the barest of foods. By 1800, the potato became the staple crop for a nearly starving population. By far the most common variety was the Irish Lumper. More than 3 million peasants

Irish Lumpers are still sold today

subsisted solely on this vegetable. The carbohydrate-rich potato also contained minerals, vitamins, and proteins that allowed families to (barely) stay alive, if not thrive. As long as the potato crop did not fail.

It did.

Between 1845 to 1852, potato blight (*Phytophthora infestans*) ravaged the crops, resulting in a famine unlike any other. Approximately one million people died and a million more emigrated, causing the population of Ireland to decline by 20 to 25 percent. The blight was especially devastating because of lack of genetic diversity. The most grievous crime of all was that Irish lands produced copious amounts of grains and beef, but all were held in the hands of the aristocracy. Irish stomachs never enjoyed this bounty; all was exported from the island.

Famine memorial in Dublin

Almost 4,000 vessels carried food from Ireland to the ports of Bristol, Glasgow, Liverpool, and London during 1847, while 400,000 Irish men, women, and children died of starvation and related diseases.[2]

During the famine years, over a million Irish arrived in the United States alone, most landing in Boston and New York. Perhaps the most well-known famine descendant was John Fitzgerald Kennedy, the great-grandson of Patrick Kennedy, a farmer from Wexford who left Ireland in 1849. By the twenty-first century, an estimated 80 million people worldwide claimed some Irish descent; which includes more than 36 million Americans who claim Irish as their primary ethnicity.[3]

The scene at Skibbereen, West Cork, 1847

Thus did the potato change the world.

Today, we can easily see how popular the potato remains. However, the next time you are sitting down to some greasy fries in a Burger Doodle restaurant, you might pause a second or two; you are munching on history.

Potatoes in a raised bed in an Ohio garden

OF NAKED LADIES AND FORGET-ME-NOTS

The Plant

Solanum tuberosum   *Potato*

All sorrow aside, potatoes are reasonably easy vegetables for the home gardener to grow. Many varieties are offered—white-, red-, and light brown-skinned forms are all available. Plant seed pieces, each containing at least two "eyes," in early spring, about a week after the last frost. Plant approximately 12 to 18 inches apart.

If soils are heavy, the use of containers or raised beds makes life a good deal easier. In the South, plant in March for June potatoes. In general, plants are more successful in northern climes than in the South. Warm conditions are not as conducive to good tuber formation. Early potatoes may be harvested in about 10 weeks, later varieties, two weeks after that. Watch for the tops of the plants to yellow before you dig, but don't wait for a hard frost, which most types cannot tolerate.

References

1. Egan, T. 2016. *The Immortal Irishman: The Irish Revolutionary Who Became an American Hero*. Houghton Mifflin Harcourt, New York
2. Kinealy, Christine. 1994. *This Great Calamity*. Gill & Macmillan

King Solomon And His Seal

A spring shade garden without Solomon's seal— a plant with handsome arching stems lined with dozens of pendulous white flowers—is simply not complete. Species native to North America, Asia, and Europe are widely available to gardeners and landscapers.

The common name is partially explained by the botanical name, *Polygonatum*, which means many knees, or many angled, referring to the many knots and swellings on the gnarled rhizome (underground stem) of the plant. The common name is thought to have come from the fact that the gnarled rhizome resembled the impressions of a royal seal. It may have been named for King Solomon, "who knew the diversities of plants and the virtues of roots, has set his seal upon them in testimony of its value to man as a medicinal root."[1] Gerard also mentioned that the root looks like the stamp of a seal but mentions "the virtue the root hath in sealing and healing up green wounds, broken bones and such like. . ."[2]

Native Solomon's seal

OF NAKED LADIES AND FORGET-ME-NOTS

Variegated Asian Solomon's seal

So, whenever I tell the story of the plant, I mention how King Solomon may have used a royal seal for his letters and proclamations, the seal likely coming from this plant. It is a good story. However, nobody under the age of fifty seems to have read about King Solomon and certainly nobody under thirty has any idea what a royal seal is. Oh well.

The Plant

Polygonatum   *Solomon's seal*

Solomon's seals are all shade tolerant. Placing them in full sun results in shorter and less desirable plants. The native species are among the most substantial and beautiful but I also love the variegated form native to Asia. It is cold hardy to USDA zone 3.

References

1. Grieve, M. 1931. *A Modern Herbal*, Harcourt, Brace & Co
2. Gerard, John, 1597. *The Herball or Generall Historie of Plantes*. Imprinted London, UK, John Norton

The Nightmare On Elm Street:
Spanish Moss

Travelers through the hot, humid states in the American Southeast cannot help but comment on the long beards of gray that hang down from many trees. Appearing almost prehistoric and kind of creepy at first sight, they are as much a part of the Southern landscape as kudzu, but far less destructive.

This plant is neither a moss nor is it Spanish. In fact, it is a flowering bromeliad, closely related to pineapples. Plants are native to Mexico, Central America, North and South America, and the Caribbean.

Many stories have been told about the origins of Spanish moss, probably the best known is the Legend of Spanish Moss. While many versions may be heard, it tells the story of a bearded Spanish brute, Gorez Goz, who bought an Indian maiden for a bar of soap. She was so frightened that she ran as fast as she could and climbed the highest tree. Just as the Spaniard was about to grab her, she jumped into the water and escaped. However, Gorez's beard became hopelessly tangled in the branches. There he died. But his beard lived forever as was known as Spanish moss.[1]

Spanish moss in July in Bluffton, South Carolina

The name is thought to have originated from the French explorers in the area as an insult to their Spanish rivals. They called it *barbe espagnol* or Spanish beard, which later became known as Spanish moss.

The Plant

Tillandsia usneoides   **Spanish moss**

These plants are really cool. The hairlike stems cling to cracks, crevices, and niches in trees and grow downward, like tinsel on a Christmas tree. They bear tiny greenish flowers and produce seed, which are dispersed through the air to other host trees. Plants are epiphytic, using the trees for support and protection and are not parasitic. They get their nutrients from the air, not their host plants. While they can drape down from almost any tree and even telephone wires, their preference is mainly live oak and bald cypress.

References

1. Ten things you should know about Spanish moss. Mental Floss. http://mentalfloss.com/article/67807/10-things-you-should-know-about-spanish-moss

Relaxing With St. John

The term "wort" has been mentioned many times under the Doctrine of Signatures (which see) but some worts deserve their own story. There are numerous species of St. John's wort (*Hypericum*), and it is likely that one or two came to be associated with St. John the Baptist, so the entire genus was thus named.

Hypericum has a calming influence when ingested, and supposedly it was one of the herbs carried by missionaries because of their great regard for St. John the Baptist.[1] The fact that it flowers around St. John's Day (June 23) also added to its common name.

Hypericum x inodorum

Later Christians came to believe it was useful to ward off evil, and could be "put out in a mannes house from whence would come no wicked spyrte therein."[1]

St. John's wort was also associated with more positive circumstances. It was said to foretell the time of a young woman's marriage, and even to indicate whom the groom would be.

OF NAKED LADIES AND FORGET-ME-NOTS

From a German legend

The young maid stole through the cottage door,
And blushed as she sought the plant of power.
'Thou silver glow-worm, oh! lend me thy light,
I must gather the mystic St. John's Wort to-night;
The wonderful herb whose leaf will decide
If the coming year shall see me a bride."

Hypericum calycinum

In America, *Hypericum* was reduced to the status of a lowly pasture weed. It was reported that even the famous naturalist John Bartram suggested it was nothing but a "pernicious weed . . . choking the grass and poisoning our horses and sheep."[2]

St. John's wort will always be associated with one of the most famous names in Christian history and has certainly not been forgotten. Today its calming properties are promoted at herbal medicine shops everywhere. It is one of the most popular over-the-counter remedies for stress and is commonly called "natural Prozac."

The Plant

Hypericum   ***St. John's wort***

Dozens of species reside under the common name but only a half dozen are available to most gardeners. Most thrive in well-drained soils and sunny locations. They tend to struggle in summers with high temperatures and high humidity, and are more common in the North than the South. Many choices are available for the gardener.

Plants are cold hardy to about USDA zone 4 to 5, depending on selection.

References

1. Larkey, S.V and Pyles, T. 1525. *Bankes Herbal*
2. Wildflower Information. Wildflower folklore. http://www.wildflowerinformation.org/WildflowerFolklore.asp

Sweetening The Air With Sweet Flag

I have grown three or four types of sweet flags in my gardens. All have handsome foliage and small, rather unremarkable flowers. I grew them as ground covers and always admired their tenacity. The leaves are somewhat scented, but hardly sweet, and they certainly could not be confused for a flag of any country.

Variegated sweet flag, A. calamus

It turns out I did not do enough digging, literally. The rhizomes are remarkably fragrant—so much so that an essential oil from the roots is still valued in the perfume industry. Essence of Calamus is used in pipe tobacco (one of the reasons pipe smoke is so much more pleasant than that of cigarettes) and has also been added to European wines. The lower stems and rhizomes, which can be dried, were historically used to scent clothes, cupboards, and even floors.[1]

Another, even more important, reason for the "sweet" moniker is that in Shakespearean Britain and long before, the custom of "rushcutting" was common.[2]

The custom seems to have begun with the cutting of *Acorus calamus. Acorus* is not a rush at all, but was called such by the person known as the "rush gatherer." Rushcutting arose from the need to reduce the smell of the packed earth floors of medieval houses.

This custom was common not only in lowly houses but also with the nobility. Queen Elizabeth seems to have been the last English monarch to have her palace strewn with rushes.[2]

Essentially, we should credit sweet flag with being one of the first accepted air fresheners.

The leaves of *Acorus calamus* resemble those of iris, which in England have been commonly known as "flags" since the fourteenth century.

Variegated short sweet flag with ranunculus

Acorus calamus   **Sweet flag**

Plants are easy to grow and are in much demand for ponds, bioswales, and consistently moist areas, where they may grow up to 4 feet tall.

The small, creamy Jack-in-the-pulpit-like flowers occur in spring. A more handsome variegated form is also available. Plants are cold hardy to USDA zone 4.

About two feet tall, *A. gramineus* is even more widespread as a garden plant. It is also known as sweet flag but has grasslike foliage. The most popular form is the variegated 'Ogon'.

References

1. Rook, E.J.S, 2002. Rook.org. *Acorus americanus, sweet flag*
http://www.rook.org/earl/bwca/nature/aquatics/acorus.html
2. George, David, *Rushbearing: a forgotten British custom*, p 17-29 IN English Parish Drama, Johnston, A. and Husken, W, Rodopi, BV, 1996

How Ladies Came To Be Wallflowers

Wallflowers seem to have gone out of fashion. Fortunately, a good deal of interest is being shown by plant breeders to enhance its vigor and show, so I am hoping that wallflowers come back in vogue.

While the original wallflowers are somewhat shy and unassuming, they never lacked for tenacity. They have been well known for hundreds of years for growing in chinks of stone walls. The herbalist and botanist Gerard wrote in 1596, "The wallflower groweth on bricke and stone walls, in the corners of churches, as also among rubbish and other such stony places everywhere."[1] This likely explains the common name.

'Citrona Orange', new breeding

A rather undignified term has also arisen based on this plant. The term "wallflower" refers to a person who has no one to dance with, or feels shy, awkward, or excluded at a function. Today, the term seems to have morphed into describing a female but that was not always the case - young men may certainly be included in this shy group. Regardless, the term refers to those shy and unassuming people sitting against a wall, as far away from the proceedings as possible. How I recall those tortuous dances as a teenager, the wall could not be far enough away.

The Plant

Erysimum   *Wallflower*

Their history as a wall plant makes two care tips obvious. Plant in full sun and provide excellent drainage. As a garden plant, breeding has been going on for years resulting in stunning colors and vigorous plants. Their somewhat rambling habit and colorful flowers are excellent for the cottage garden look.

A few species are cold hardy to about USDA zone 7, but most should be treated as annuals almost everywhere in the United States and Canada.

Tulipmania—The First Financial Bubble

Something was out of control during the 1630s in Holland. Thousands of normally sober, hardworking Dutch citizens from every walk of life were caught up in an extraordinary frenzy of buying and selling . . . tulip bulbs!

Rich Dutch merchants coming to the town of Alkmaar, about 25 miles north of Amsterdam, were there to conduct business—not in grain, spices, or fish but rather in tulip bulbs. Tulips were so scarce and in such demand that some traders were buying and selling single bulbs for hundreds, even thousands of guilders and building paper fortunes of forty to sixty thousand guilders in a year or two.

Tulipa 'Angelique'

OF NAKED LADIES AND FORGET-ME-NOTS

How did this happen?

In 1593, tulips were introduced to Holland from Turkey. The novelty of the new flower made it widely sought after, resulting in extraordinary prices. When the mosaic virus occurred that caused random "flames" on the petals and made them even more unique, prices skyrocketed again. In the 1630s, the rush to buy took off.

In a recorded auction in Alkmaar on February 5, 1637, some single bulbs sold for over 1,000 guilders each. When the final bulb had been sold, over 9,000 guilders had passed hands. This was, quite literally, a fortune in 1637.[1]

What do these prices mean? Perhaps the following table will put the craziness in perspective:

The basic currency in Holland was the guilder. One guilder equaled 20 stuviers. Some typical costs in the 1630s:[2]

½ stuvier	Cost of a tankard of beer
18 stuviers	Daily wage of an Amsterdam cloth-shearer (about 250 guilders/year)
13 guilders	Price for a ton of herring
60 guilders	Price for 40 gallons of French brandy
250 guilders	Annual earnings of a carpenter
1500 guilders	Annual earnings of a middle-class merchant
1600 guilders	Rembrandt's fee for his masterpiece *The Night Watch* (1642)
3000 guilders	Annual earnings of a well-off merchant
5200 guilders	Highest reliably attested price paid for a tulip bulb (1637)

Even with prices out of control, people began to speculate on the tulip market, which was believed to have no limits. Soon, prices were rising so fast and high that people were trading their land, savings, and anything else they could liquidate to obtain more bulbs. Many believed they could sell them to

Tulipa 'Ballerina'

hapless, unenlightened foreigners and reap enormous profits. It was hard to blame them as they watched already inflated prices go up twenty-fold in a single month.

As happens in speculative bubbles, some prudent investors decided to sell and take their profits. A domino effect of progressively lower prices occurred as everyone tried to sell, while few were buying. The price dove, causing panic.

Dealers refused to honor contracts and people lost their homes, their land, and their savings for some rather worthless bulbs. This was the first recorded instance of a financial bubble, and certainly was not the last.

Tulipa   ***Tulip***

A tulip is botanically an annual, meaning that it must make a new bulb every year. Conditions in some parts of the world, such as Holland, are conducive to this lifecycle. However in many areas in this country, especially in the American South, soil temperatures are too high and new bulbs do not form. In such places, bulbs should be replaced each year for the best show. Unlike prices those many years ago, tulips are inexpensive and the show is well worth the dollars spent.

If planting in an area when tulips come back each year, place in full sun. Planting in the fall provides the cool temperatures the flowers need to break free from the bulb and arise from the soil. If you expect the tulips to return the next spring, allow the leaves to go yellow if possible. However, if you tire of the foliage, wait a few weeks and trim the top half of the leaves away. They will do just fine. None of this matters if you replace bulbs every year.

References

1. Dash, Mike, 1999. *Tulipomania, The Story of the World's Most Coveted Flower & the Extraordinary Passions it Aroused.* Three Rivers Press, New York
2. Goldar, Anne, 2007. *Tulipmania, Money, Honor, and Knowledge in the Dutch Golden Age,* University of Chicago Press

Who Was Sweet William

Sweet William is one of the many plants in the genus *Dianthus*, otherwise known as pinks (which see) and carnation. The flowers are sweet smelling but I have always been curious why the name "William" was part of the common name.

A number of explanations may be found, but none are verified. It may honor the eighteenth-century Prince William, Duke of Cumberland, perhaps for his victory at putting down the Scottish highlanders at the Battle of Culloden in 1746. If so, the sweet moniker is particularly ironic. In the aftermath of the battle, Cumberland and his forces sought out, captured, and jailed or executed many of the remaining clan leaders. Sweet William he was not!

One of the first mentions of the common name was in Gerard's *Herball*,[1] first published in 1597, almost 150 years before Culloden. A strong argument can thus be made that it was named to commemorate Gerard's contemporary, William Shakespeare.[2]

'Coral Magic' sweet William

OF NAKED LADIES AND FORGET-ME-NOTS

The Plant

Dianthus barbatus   **Sweet William**

Sweet Williams are easy plants for growing in the sunny garden or in containers on the deck. Many colors are available. The older cultivars were biennial, meaning they were vegetative the first year and flowered the next spring. Today's newer choices are hybrids and may persist either as annuals or as short-lived perennials. I treat them as two-year plants at best.

References

1. Phillips, H. (1829). *Flora Historica*, E. Lloyd & Son
2. Gerard, John, 1597. *The Herball or Generall Historie of Plantes*. Imprinted London, UK, John Norton

Trout Lily

A plant that goes by names like trout lily, fawn lily, yellow adder's tongue, and dog-tooth violet must have caught a naturalist's attention somewhere down the line. The first two names are in reference to the mottled foliage; the gray-green leaves resemble the coloring of trout, in particular brook trout, and young fawns. Plants grow from pointed corms that have also been said to resemble dog's teeth. Dog-tooth violet is another common name, but it's generally associated with the European species, *Erythronium dens-canis*. Plants produce violet flowers.

The mottled leaves of trout lily actually do resemble the skin of the brook trout

The Plant

Erythronium americanum   *Trout lily, fawn lily*

Plants are early spring ephemerals—emerging, flowering, and disappearing within a month's time. They are found in colonies in eastern North American deciduous woodlands from Canada to north Georgia.

Dog teeth-like corms

The subtly handsome foliage and the beautiful yellow flowers are like magnets to the naturalist and gardener. Plants take years to flower and in any given colony most will be nonflowering. If you want to grow them, buy corms from a reputable vendor—do not dig from the woods—and plant in shady areas of the garden. They will slowly spread over the years and, if you are lucky, you may notice a few more each spring.

Plants are cold hardy to about USDA zone 3.

Plants of trout lily in a Georgia garden

Do Skunk Cabbages Really Smell?

I recall walking with a group through a wonderful spring garden replete with sweet-smelling shrubs and handsome flowers. As we rounded a bend noses started twitching and people started commenting. Something smelly was definitely up ahead. As gardeners, we couldn't wait to see the source but as we turned the corner, it was obvious we were going to have to get in line. The skunk cabbage was blooming and the flies, beetles, and their entire families had already arrived.

Skunk cabbage, early spring

The flowers have a spathe and spadix, similar to other members of the Jack-in-the-pulpit family (which see). And, as many plants in that family do, they release an odor attractive to pollinators. As they mature, this odor intensifies and the spathe opens to allow pollinators such as flies and carrion beetles to enter and pollinate the flowers.[1]

It is the rather unpleasant odor then that accounts for part of its common name. The smell is a mechanism for the plant to attract those pollinators who are attracted to rotting meat. The foliage is large and somewhat cabbagelike.

In addition to its massive stink, skunk cabbage also has the remarkable ability to produce heat; the space around it is often thawed even when the ground is frozen. One of the side effects of this mini-furnace is that the smell is carried away from the plant on the rising warm air, thus attracting even more pollinators.

Skunk cabbage through the snow

The Plant

Symplocarpus foetidus	Skunk cabbage

Unless you are populating a wet area, it is doubtful you will be gardening with skunk cabbage. In fact, while it may be part of the diet of numerous pollinators, it is poisonous to most mammals. It's probably not a good idea for Fido to be chewing on it.

Plants are native in eastern Canada and the northeastern United States, west to Minnesota, and southeast to Tennessee and North Carolina. Western skunk cabbage (*Lysichiton americanus*), which has yellow flowers, is found in the western states, British Columbia, and north to Alaska.

References

1. National Wildlife Federation. *Skunk cabbage*. http://www.nwf.org/Wildlife/Wildlife-Library/Plants/Skunk-Cabbage.aspx

The Toad Lily And Its Warts

Most gardeners know *Tricyrtis* as toad lily. That is fine, but wart flower may even be a more appropriate, and certainly more descriptive moniker. If you want people to remember this plant, remark on the beauty of toad lily, and then ask, "What did your Grandmother tell you about handling toads?"

I can almost guarantee you that they will chant - in unison, "Toads give you warts!" It is amazing how such tales endure.

Once the shouting has diminished, slowly turn over a flower and show the three "warts" on the back. They will ooh and aah, and never forget the plant. Not only you but anyone who hears you tell the story of the wart flower will repeat it to unsuspecting friends.

Toad lily is the more common appellation given to *Tricyrtis*. There are a good number of stories running around out there. Some are as simple as the color of the flowers being somewhat similar to the color of toads.

Note the "warts" on the back of the flower

Another somewhat more interesting story, has its origins in the early 1970s. It is based on a *National Geographic* article about the long-lost Tasaday tribe in the rain forests of the Philippines. It was an unprecedented discovery of a lost people, and subsequently widely reported.

Photos were taken and books were written about their rituals. One of these was to crush the leaves and rub the juice of *Tricyrtis* on their hands claiming that toads and frogs would be attracted to their scent and be easier to catch. Thus the name "toad lily."

Many people argue that the entire story, including the existence of such a tribe, was a hoax. For some different viewpoints on this quite lively story, see the references.[1, 2]

We'll always have the toad lily, but for me, I'm sticking with wart flower.

Wartflowers (toad lilies) in early September

The Plant

Tricyrtis   *Wartflower, toad lily*

Plants don't usually flower until late summer and into fall. They are handsome additions to the shade garden, but morning sun enhances plant performance. Dozens of hybrids are available, including those with variegated foliage. If for no other reason, I grow some plants to be able to entertain people about warts. After all, how else can we keep Grandma's stories alive?

References

1. Museum of Hoaxes. *The stone-age Tasaday.* http://hoaxes.org/archive/permalink/the_stone-age_tasaday
2. Paghat. *Samurai toad lily.* http://www.paghat.com/toadlily.html

Woundwort And
The Warrior Achilles

Ask a group of gardeners about the common name of *Achillea* and without hesitation most will reply "yarrow." However, they likely would not know that yarrow was believed to possess many properties, was long associated with magic and witchcraft, and was often strewn across the threshold of a house to ward against evil spirits.

Yarrow was a plant of Venus and, as such, was frequently mentioned where matters of love were concerned. One love charm called for yarrow to be placed under the pillow and the following poem to be read. If the charm were successful, one's future husband or wife would appear in a dream.[1]

'Peachy Seduction' woundwort

Thou pretty herb of Venus' tree,
Thy true name it is Yarrow;
Now who my bosom friend must be,
Pray tell thou me to-morrow.

Yarrow is derived from the old English *gearwe*, which simply meant "yarrow." Such a name gives no hint as to some of the properties of this most interesting plant. Given its long history, it is not surprising that other common names exist.

The Burning of Troy—*oil painting by Johann Georg Trautmann*

It is said that the great Greek warrior Achilles, after whom the genus is named, used a poultice of yarrow leaves to staunch minor wounds of his soldiers at the Battle of Troy. The concoction became known as woundwort ("wort" signifies some use for the plant, see Doctrine of Signatures) and while yarrow is the name most commonly used today, woundwort is surely more descriptive. Plants are still used to treat cuts, scratches, rashes, and burns, and to stop minor bleeding. If you wish to test its efficacy, check out the video on making a yarrow poultice.[2]

By the way, historians are still arguing if there ever was a Battle of Troy, or if Achilles ever set foot on the earth. So while woundwort is a terrific common name, the story should be filed in the "definite maybe" drawer.

The Plant

Achillea millefolium   **Woundwort, yarrow**

Plants are available in a diverse range of flower colors and plant heights, from 8 inches to 3 feet in height. Place in full sun. For the larger selections, some staking may be necessary, especially in the South. Cut back all woundworts after flowering; flowering may occur again. This is an excellent perennial for gardeners almost anywhere, and it's cold hardy at least to USDA zone 4.

Plants bloom in late spring and early summer. They make excellent cut flowers to bring into the house. Not only that, they are particularly drought-tolerant.

References

1. Silverman, M. 1977. *A City Herbal. Lore, legend & uses of common weeds. 192 p.* Ash Tree Publishing, Woodstock, New York
2. Native Survival Community, 2010. *Yarrow wound dressing.* www.youtube.com/watch?v=ejhe8rsvl88

'Rose Beauty' with dahlias

What's A Culver, Anyway?

I have admired Culver's root for years. It is robust, flowers well, possesses excellent foliage, and is an American native. What's not to like? However, I was curious about the common name. I wondered if there was some old English meaning to the term "culver" or whether it had something to do with a culvert, or perhaps it was a design on the root itself. Once I started looking into it, it was, of course, option "D"—none of the above.

Culver's root

It turns out that the plant, particularly the roots, were quite useful medicinally, employed to treat problems of the gallbladder and liver as well as constipation and colitis. Native American tribes in Missouri and Delaware, such as the Ojibwa or the Chippewa tribes and the Seneca Indians, used the plant for medicinal or purification rituals.[1,2]

The use of this herb as a laxative and detoxifying agent was adopted early by the European settlers. Later the herb was used as a remedy against liver diseases and to stimulate bile production.[1]

'Pink Glow' Culver's root

Its first recorded use in North America was in 1716 when Cotton Mather, a well-known Puritan minister, sought a remedy for his daughter's tuberculosis and asked for the plant. Unfortunately, nothing was effective and she died soon thereafter.[1]

Although the plant was not commonly recommended, one person seems to have prescribed the root repeatedly over many years, far more often than others. His name was Dr. Culver, and the plant was named for him.

Little is known about Dr. Culver other than that he was an American physician who lived in the early 1700s. He often prescribed the bitter roots for purgative purposes. The plant is still sold today and frequently found in herbal medicines. The root contains eptandrin, a powerful emetic, and should be used with caution.

Veronicastrum virginicum   *Culver's root*

This is one of the easiest plants to grow, at home in the formal bed as well as meadow garden. Provide full sun and decent drainage, and plants will reward you with 4- to 5-foot-tall stems and handsome white spears of flowers. A number of nativars are available with pink to rose flowers, such as 'Pink Glow'. It's hardy to USDA zones 3 to 8.

References

1. Vogel, Virgil J. 1970. American Indian Medicine. University of Oklahoma Press, Norman, OK (p 297)
2. Densmore, Frances. 1973. *How Indians Use Wild Plants for Food, Medicine & Crafts* (originally published in the *"Forty-fourth Annual Report of the Bureau of American Ethnology to the Secretary of the Smithsonian Institution, 1926-1927"*). Dover Press

Poke Salad Annie

Of all the "weeds" I encountered during my initiation to the South from Canuck-land, I was most fascinated with the native pokeweed. Plants grew at a rocket pace, attaining heights over 5 feet tall by mid-June. Their red stems as they emerged from the ground, the don't-mess-with-me stature, and the intense red berries made this an intriguing specimen. All in all, the plant was surprisingly attractive.

It turns out that the fruit is a food source for many birds but highly poisonous to many mammals, including humans. In fact, it can be a malicious plant indeed. I was not truly aware of the potential severity of pokeweed to cause dermatitis until my friend Jim Sollecito showed me his arm. He had briefly come in contact with the sap and suffered third-degree burns. After a month, it was still blistered.

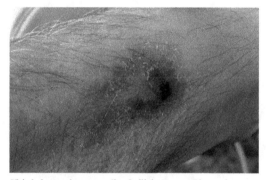

Third-degree burns on Jim Sollicito's arm. Photo shot one month after contacting pokeweed.

I also read story after story about children eating the berries and becoming violently ill. So, between skin scorching and stomach retching, you can imagine how surprised I was to learn that Southerners actually eat the stuff! Apparently, the boiled young leaves are quite tasty and are known as poke salet. This delicacy was available on the grocery shelf until about 2000. I knew then that my initiation would be a long one indeed.

Poke greens were distributed by the Allen Canning Company of Siloam Springs, Arkansas, until 2000.

There is a rich history about pokeweed; one of the most readable accounts is by Allison Adams from Decatur, Georgia.[1]

Pokeberry has been the subject of a couple of interesting stories as well. It seems that some supporters of James Polk, the eleventh president of the United States, mistakenly thought pokeberry was named for the president. As such, they would often wear sprigs of pokeweed on their lapels or around their necks in his honor.[2] Hmm, sounds like lack of political brains is nothing new after all.

And of course, who could think of pokeweed without humming a bar or two from Tony Joe White's ballad "Poke Salad Annie" about the lifestyle of a poor rural Southern girl. Pretty good song; it reached #8 on Billboard's Hot 100 in 1969. It is still being sung. One of the more memorable performances was by Tony Joe White and the Foo Fighters on the *Late Show with David Letterman* in October 2014.

However, strange as the history may be, I still could not figure out if the poke of pokeweed had to do with the way it

American pokeweed

aggressively poked through the soil or the fact that it pokes its nose everywhere. The first instance of it being called pokeweed was in the early 1700s, resulting from its use as a dye. The name likely arose from the Algonquin word for red dye, *poughkone* (also mentioned in the story of bloodroot, which see), a plant used to extract dyes. Over time, it became known as pokeweed.

The Plant

Phytolacca americana   **Pokeweed**

Although the plant seems more rooted in the South, it is native into the Midwest and parts of the Northeast as well. While I suppose it could be used as an ornamental, it is a plant to see, enjoy its history, and leave for the wildlife.

Other species of *Phytolacca* are quite ornamental and find their ways routinely into European gardens.

References

1. Adams, A., 2011. *A mess of poke*. Southern Spaces. Oct 17. https://southernspaces.org/2011/mess-poke
2. Johnson, T.W., *Out my backdoor: the wondrous pokeberry*. Georgia Department of Natural resources. http://georgiawildlife.com/node/2793
3. Online Etymology Dictionary. *Poke*

The Hooker's Lips

I had to include hooker's lips because the name is so fitting for the plant, but truth be known, there is nothing common about this plant at all. In fact, you will never see it unless you have a conservatory or greenhouse and you are a crazy plant collector. Many plants have names that perfectly describe their flowers; some that quickly come to mind are musical note plant, balloon flower, and eyeball plant. This is another whose flowers scream their name.

They remind me of the bright red wax candy lips that my six-year-old son came home with from school one day. It was Halloween, and they seemed perfect. I can't exactly remember who he was that night, Luke Skywalker or the Lone Ranger, but I do remember his ridiculous red lips.

The Plant

Psychotria elata   ***Hooker's lips***

Referred to as Latin America's kissable flower, the lips are actually two bracts (like dogwood) that remain only for a short time. After they fade, the white flowers appear between them.

Bracts of hooker's lips open to reveal the white flowers

If you actually find seeds or a plant (they are endangered as deforestation continues in their native territory—rain forests of South and Central America), purchase them. Plants perform best in a container on a partially shaded deck or patio. Bring them inside when temperatures fall near 40 degrees F in autumn.

The Unruly Obedient Plant

I recall the first time someone told me about obedient plant. "Just push the flowers up or down and they obey your touch. They stay put."

I did so. Perhaps it was just me, but those darn flowers did not obey at all. I kept pushing; they kept disobeying. This was one sham of a common name, I thought.

Then one day I tried again. Instead of pushing the flowers up and down, I gently shoved a flower to one side. It stayed! I did it again and as each flower obeyed, confidence in my leadership abilities grew.[1] Having had my share of unruly students, unruly administrators, and unruly grandchildren, I was finally able to enjoy a little obedience. I am easily mollified.

Other stories of why the plant is called obedient plant are out there, but now that I have mastered the skill, this is the story I am sticking with.[1]

Handsome flowers of obedient plant

The Plant

Physostegia virginiana   **Obedient plant**

This is one of the easiest plants to grow, but obedient in the garden it is not! It is considered aggressive by all, and downright invasive by many gardeners. If I am planting it, I generally use a deep container, and enjoy it with other companions on my deck or veranda. In the garden it has a tendency to wander, and, in a few years, you will likely be sharing it with unsuspecting neighbors.

Having said that, it is a beautiful native plant, useful for its pink color and as a cut flower to enjoy indoors. Plants are hardy at least to USDA zone 4.

A number of cultivars such as 'Miss Manners' are shorter and less aggressive, and easier to love than the species.

References

1. Armitage, A. 2016. *Obedient plant being obedient*
https://www.youtube.com/watch?v=nT-xofkgL38&feature=em-upload_owner

Plucking Yew

As this is the last entry in the book, I saved one of the better stories for the end. All sorts of outrageous tales can be found when researching common names, and no, the yew was not named after a female sheep.

The derivation of yew is thought to come from a Welsh word *eugh,* for "rough wood." The Celtic word *iw* and the Germanic *iwo* both refer to verdure, meaning evergreen. Other languages are also thought to play a part in its name, but like many common names, the origin is elusive.

However, that it was used in making bows is not in doubt. The wood was prized for its strength and pliability and

Crecy village sign depicting longbow archers

the famous English longbow was generally made from the yew (particularly *Taxus baccata*).

An interesting story connects a number of common expressions involving the yew and the crossbow. There is no truth to this story at all but we need a little creativity and humor in the world of horticulture, so here goes. The following story was told on the

The English (Irish) yew

NPR radio show *Car Talk* in 1996. I have no shame, so I tell it often.

The Battle of Agincourt (1415) was one of the many battles between the English and French during the Hundred Years' War. The English were badly outnumbered but won the battle for many reasons, not the least of which was the employment of thousands of archers deploying the famous longbow. One of the terms for drawing back the bow was "plucking yew" and the English taunted the French by repeatedly yelling, "We can still pluck yew." Pluck yew is relatively difficult to say and it is said that the letter "f" may have found its way into the expression and been changed over time. The person from whom the archers bought their feathers was known as a "pheasant plucker" (another rather difficult term to say rapidly) and it is claimed that the symbolic gesture of "giving the bird" arose from these two types of pluckers.[1]

Who says creativity is not alive and well?

The Plant

Taxus   *Yew*

Yews are one of the most popular evergreens in the landscape, used as foundation plantings, as hedges, and as large specimens. All parts of the plant are poisonous, and incidents of livestock and human fatalities are not uncommon. They're cold hardy to USDA zone 3, but they do poorly in the Southern states.

References

1. About.com, *Pluck Yew, the origin of the finger.* http://urbanlegends.about.com/od/errata/fl/Pluck-Yew-The-Origin-of-The-Finger.htm

Foliage and fruit

Index of Common Names

Index of Common Names cont'd

Index of Common Names cont'd

Index of Botanical Names and Their Common Name

Achillea millefolium	woundwort, yarrow
Achillea ptarmica	sneezewort
Aconitum	monkshood, wolfsbane
Acorus calamus	sweet flag, sweet rush
Actaea	baneberry, doll's eyes
Agave americana	century plant
Ajuga reptans	bugleweed
Alcea	hollyhock
Alchemilla mollis	lady's mantle, dewdrops
Amaranthus caudatus	love-lies-bleeding
Antirrhinum majus	snapdragon
Apocynum cannabinum	dogbane, Indian hemp
Arisaema triphyllum	Indian turnip, Jack-in-the-pulpit, parson-in-the-pulpit
Asclepias tuberosa	butterfly weed, pleurisy root
Asimina triloba	pawpaw, Indiana banana
Asplenium	spleenwort
Baptisia	false indigo
Bergenia	elephant ears, piqsqueak
Cardamine	toothwort
Cardiospermum halicacabum	love-in-a-puff
Centaurea cyanus	bachelor's buttons
Chamerion angustifolium	bombweed, fireweed
Clematis	old man's beard, traveler's joy, virgin's bower
Cornus	dogwood
Datura stramonium	devil's weed, hell's bells, jimsonweed, locoweed, thorn apple, trumpet weed
Daucus carota	carrot, Queen Anne's lace

Index of Botanical Names and Their Common Name cont'd

Delosperma	ice plant
Dianthus	pinks
Dianthus barbatus	sweet William
Dicentra cucullaria	Dutchman's breeches, eardrops, fairy candles, little boys' breeches
Dictamnus albus	gas plant
Digitalis	foxglove
Dipsacus sativus	teasel
Dracunculus vulgaris	carrion lily, voodoo lily
Echinocactus grusonii	mother-in-law cushion
Epimedium	barrenwort, bishop's hat, horny goat weed
Erysimum	wallflower
Erythronium americanum	fawn lily, trout lily
Eutrochium perfoliatum	boneset
Eutrochium purpureum	Joe Pye weed
Euonymus americanus	hearts-a-bursting, strawberry plant
Galium	bedstraw, lady's bedstraw, sweet woodruff
Gomphocarpus physocarpus	balloon plant, cotton bush, hairy balls, swan plant
Gypsophila paniculata	baby's breath
Helenium autumnale	Helen flower, sneezeweed
Hepatica	liverwort
Heracleum mantegazzianum	hogweed
Hesperis matronalis	dame's rocket, dame's violet, mother-of-the-evening
Hibiscus mutabilis	Confederate rose
Hypericum	St. John's wort

Index of Botanical Names and Their Common Name cont'd

Pleopeltis polypodioides	resurrection fern
Polygonatum	Solomon's seal
Psychotria elata	hooker's lips
Pulmonaria	lungwort
Rudbeckia hirta	black-eyed Susan
Sanguinaria canadensis	bloodroot, puccoon
Sansevieria trifasciata	mother-in-law tongue, snake plant
Saponaria	bouncing Bet, soapwort
Scabiosa caucasica	pincushion flower, scabious
Sempervivum	chicks, cats and kittens, hens and chicks
Solanum melongena	aubergine, eggplant
Solanum tuberosum	potato
Spilanthes acmella	eyeball plant, toothache plant
Stachys byzantina	betony, lamb's ears, wooly betony, rabbit's ears, donkey's ears
Symplocarpus foetidus	skunk cabbage
Taxus	yew
Tillandsia usneoides	Spanish moss
Tradescantia	spiderwort, wandering Jew
Tricyrtis	toad lily, wart flower
Tulipa	tulip
Veronicastrum virginicum	Culver's root
Viola tricolor	Johnny jump up, heartsease
Vitex agnus-castus	chaste tree, monk's pepper

Photo Credits

Page 2: The Gazette-Democrat

Page 9: Polly Brennan

Page 14: Gottscho-Schleisner Collection/Public Domain

Page 15: Vincent Simeone

Page 17: Wikimedia Commons

Page 19: Holger Casselmann/ Wikimedia Commons

Page 21: Tavia Cathcart Brown

Page 23: Boneset drawing-Culbreath, D./ Public Domain, Bonset in a
meadow-RA Nonemacher/Wikimedia Commons

Page 27: World Carrot Museum

Page 28: Doctor Carrot poster-Wikimedia Commons/Public Domain,
Carrots ready to harvest- Daderot/Wikimedia Commons

Page 31: Norbert Nagel/ Wikimedia Commons

Page 33: Dr. Tim Smalley

Page 54: Both photos-Public Domain

Page 58: Andrei Suslov/ Wikimedia Commons

Page 71: Prairie Moon Nursery

Page 76: Lucarelli/ Wikimedia Commons

Page 83: Wikimedia Commons/ Public Domain

Page 84: Wikimedia Commons/ Public Domain

Page 89: Vincent Simeone

Page 92: Richerman at en.wikipedia

Page 100: Zdeněk Vojtěch H. / Wikimedia Commons

Page 106: Rob Hille/ Wikimedia Commons/ Public Domain

Page 113: Wikimedia Commons

Page 117: Libuše Marková

Page 121: Cramers Farm, Mount Joy, PA

Page 140: Scott Bauer/ Wikimedia Commons/ Public Domain

Page 143: Wikimedia Commons

Page 147: Wikimedia Commons

Page 148: Gustave Doré/ Public Domain

Page 159: H. Zell/ Wikimedia Commons

Page 165: Jrosenberry1/ Wikimedia Commons

Photo Credits cont'd

About the Author

Dr. Allan Armitage is well-known as an award-winning writer, speaker, and researcher throughout the world. In addition to 15 books, he's written hundreds of academic and industry papers, as well as a unique monthly column for "Greenhouse Grower" for over 30 years. No column has ever been repeated! He is an Emeritus Profesor of Horticultutre at the University of Georgia (retired 2014). His app for smartphones and tablets, "Armitage's Greatest Perennials & Annuals," serves as a bridge between industry and consumer and is popular for home gardeners and industry professionals alike. He holds academic degrees from McGill University, Canada, University of Guelph, Canada and Michigan State University, USA. Allan has Introduced over 20 plants to the gardeing community, including best-sellers Verbena 'Homestead Purple' and 'Margarita' ornamental sweet potato. He's an invited lecturer in Canada, the United States, Portugal, Colombia, New Zealand, Australia, and Europe and is in constant demand. He has visited research and production centers throughout the world and studies annuals, perennials, cut flowers, and greenhouse crops in various climates. His tour company, Garden Vistas, has organized tours to the Great Gardens of the World every year for over 25 years. Learn more and keep in touch at *www.allanarmitage.net.*

CPSIA information can be obtained
at www.ICGtesting.com
Printed in the USA
JSHW011715220819
1170JS00003BA/4